THE MINDFULNESS WORKBOOK
FOR DEPRESSION

THE MINDFULNESS WORKBOOK FOR
DEPRESSION

Effective Mindfulness Strategies
to Cultivate Positivity from the Inside Out

YOON IM KANE, LCSW, CGP

ROCKRIDGE
PRESS

For general information on our other products and services or to obtain technical support, please contact our Customer Care Department within the United States at (866) 744-2665, or outside the United States at (510) 253-0500.

Rockridge Press publishes its books in a variety of electronic and print formats. Some content that appears in print may not be available in electronic books, and vice versa.

Interior and Cover Designer: Peatra Jariya
Art Producer: Janice Ackerman
Editors: Crystal Nero and Nicky Montalvo
Production Manager: Jose Olivera
Production Editor: Melissa Edeburn

Cover Illustration: TairA/shutterstock.com.
Author Photo: © 2020 Romer Pedron.

ISBN: Print 978-1-64739-663-3
Ebook 978-1-64739-479-0

R0

To Mom and Dad,

> who taught me that hope is a
> seed that can take root and

To Arben,

> who taught me that true, loving
> partnership is the soil that
> makes everything possible

To my patients,

> who taught me about the
> hard-won fruits of bravery and
> resilience

CONTENTS

viii   Introduction

1   Chapter One: The Connection Between Mindfulness and Depression

13   Chapter Two: Beginner's Mind

35   Chapter Three: Non-Judgment

55   Chapter Four: Acceptance

73   Chapter Five: Patience

89   Chapter Six: Trust

107   Chapter Seven: Non-Striving

129   Chapter Eight: Letting Go

151   Chapter Nine: Onward, Upward

155   Resources

158   References

159   Index

INTRODUCTION

I stumbled on my first lesson in mindfulness as a six-year-old, growing up in a small village just outside the demilitarized zone in South Korea. One summer day I was awoken by shrieks, squeals, and then laughter. My curiosity was piqued when I heard yelling and cheers outside. I threw my covers off, jumped out of bed, and ran to the window. I watched, transfixed, as village kids jumped around in a frenzy over a rusty bike they had discovered in an American military base dumpster.

The kids were immersed in pure delight. They egged one another on, helping push and hold the bike as they took turns pedaling around. I was captivated by the peeling pink flower decals, faded tassels, and rusty banana seat. The rust and decay added a touch of toughness and grit.

I raced out the door and stood a little outside the circle of kids, watching. I wanted so badly to take a turn on the bike and join in on all the fun. But I was shy, embarrassed at the thought of failing in front of everyone, and scared of getting hurt. I went to my grandfather, who said, "Instead of imagining how hard and scary it's going to be, pay attention to how the kids ride the bike, and come back and tell me all about it."

The next day, I went out to do exactly what he told me. I watched the other kids and noticed for the first time how they got on the bike, balanced, pedaled, and stopped. I went back to my grandfather and shared what I'd seen. He said, "Now that you understand how they do it, try taking a turn just sitting on the bike. You can ask a friend to push you, just a little bit."

I went back and asked one of my friends to help. I sat on the bike and fell over a couple of times, but it was fun because I wasn't going very fast and I ended up giggling every time I fell. Emboldened, I returned to my grandfather and asked him how to get moving. He said, "Instead of worrying about how far or how long you're going to stay on, focus your attention on where you want to go and pedal."

So I did. And after a few attempts, I fell and scraped my knee. Dejected, I went back to my grandfather and confessed that I didn't think I could ride a bike. He said patiently, "You've been working hard. Give yourself time to rest and then go back out there and try again when you're ready."

I took my grandfather's advice and rested until I felt the itch to try again. Before I knew it, I was back on that rusty banana seat, kids trailing behind me, grinning ear to ear with joy and exhilaration.

All these years later, even with 20 years of practicing mindfulness meditation and psychotherapy, I still remember my grandfather's wise words whenever I find myself in a difficult moment. I now realize that my grandfather's bike lesson was an introduction to the concept of mindfulness. Without lecturing, he taught me to be aware of my thoughts and feelings and to focus on what's happening in the moment, putting aside judgment and the fear of what might happen next.

Everyone has a unique way of being in the world. You can move through this workbook to discover and experience your own way of using the ideas and practices of mindfulness. In fact, that's what I like about mindfulness: You don't have to be or feel anything other than where you are in this moment. Simply start with one breath at a time.

CHAPTER ONE

THE CONNECTION BETWEEN MINDFULNESS AND DEPRESSION

What Is Mindfulness?

Simply put, mindfulness is the practice of directing one's attention to what is happening in the present moment, with the intention of acknowledging whatever arises without pushing it away or judging. It's an essential life skill that can benefit anyone. And for those of us who live with depression, it's a game-changer.

Using mindfulness to get in touch with the present moment can be an incredibly powerful act. When we do this, we build self-awareness and clarity that empowers us to break through depression-related negative thought patterns and emotional distress. As you'll learn in this book, you can cultivate mindfulness through a formal practice like meditation, through reflective activities like journaling, or through simple exercises focused on your breathing. When you make mindfulness a consistent part of your day, you build a valuable supportive relationship with yourself that you can count on and come back to no matter what challenges arise.

If you've never settled your mind enough to become aware of your current thoughts and feelings, you're missing out on a superpower you didn't know you had. Now is the time to learn to use it!

Why Choose Mindfulness?

Mindfulness isn't an esoteric philosophy. It's a capacity that we all have and a practical tool that can help shift one's state of mind in a healthy direction. Here are three important qualities of mindfulness that make it so useful for people living with depression:

Mindfulness is available to everyone. You don't need to be in a particular place, or use any special equipment, to practice mindfulness. It's also not necessary to study its roots in Buddhism or other spiritual traditions in order to reap its benefits. In fact, you really only need your mind and your breath—two things you carry with you at all times. You can practice mindfulness anywhere, anytime; you could even be doing it as you're reading this very sentence! Mindfulness is a method for bringing awareness to what's happening in the moment, at any moment.

Mindfulness is an antidote for chronic discontent. Humans have an unparalleled capacity to worry about the future and regret the past. And the modern world we live in offers a constant deluge of information that gives us plenty to worry about, leading to anxious thoughts and the chronic dissatisfaction that's at the root of many feelings associated with depression. Mindfulness provides essential tools for managing that information overload in a healthy way. Through mindfulness, you notice when your mind is worrying about the future or regretting the past, freeing you to make the choice to reconnect with what's happening right here, right now.

Mindfulness connects you with your body. Our bodies are constantly aware of what's going on around us, taking in information and experiences, and reacting to things we're not fully conscious of. From an upset stomach to a tension headache, our bodies provide us with physical clues that give us information about obscured emotions we need to attend to. Practicing mindfulness teaches us to pay attention to our breathing; by doing this, we slow down and synchronize our minds and bodies. We get better at noticing the connection between our thoughts, our feelings, and our physical state, which allows us to take better care of ourselves.

The Principles of Mindfulness

Mindfulness has seven principles to help you build resilience and put you on the path to depression recovery. These principles were first outlined by Jon Kabat-Zinn, PhD, whose mindfulness-based stress reduction (MBSR) program brought attention to mindfulness as a tool for mental health. These seven principles help frame and structure your learning and can be implemented at your own pace. They describe the mindsets you are working toward.

Beginner's mind. Choosing to approach an experience with a beginner's mind is allowing yourself to clear away your preconceived ideas, "shoulds," and "what ifs" and instead cultivate an attitude of openness, curiosity, and eagerness to learn. Beginner's mind calls you to leave behind your assumptions and fears, making space for a new approach.

Non-judgment. Judgment can be a protective act to fend off potential rejection, embarrassment, and criticisms: We feel safest when we are our harshest critic. Yet the harder we are on ourselves, the more likely we are to feel lonely, isolated, and stagnant. Non-judgment is the act of removing evaluations and measurements and observing our experiences with neutrality. Instead of judging, we treat ourselves and others with compassion, cultivating openness, connection, and tolerance.

Acceptance. Each of us has feelings and experiences that are difficult to accept. But when we come to understand that we don't have to be anyone other than who we are, we can learn to accept ourselves. And the more okay we are with ourselves, the more deeply we can connect with others. Acceptance is learning to embrace unwanted feelings and experiences because they're an unavoidable part of living. The first step is to welcome our own imperfections and recognize our basic goodness. Our imperfections make us who we are; by accepting them, we embrace our full selves. Acceptance allows us to confidently engage with life with an open and generous heart.

Patience. Life can move really fast; we can get caught up in all the things we want to be doing without really being present in what we *are* doing. Patience is allowing experiences to unfold on their schedule, not ours. It's willingness to spend time on things that are really hard. It's allowing ourselves to take as much time as we need with all our feelings.

Trust. Trust isn't automatic—it happens through consistency. We typically think of trust as something we build with other people, but it's actually a quality we need to build with ourselves. In the context of mindfulness, trust means having conviction in one's inner knowing or wisdom. The first step to developing a trusting relationship with yourself can be mindful awareness of what you're feeling in this moment. Trust is a result of showing up for yourself, spending time listening to your inner voice, and learning to have faith in your ability to meet your own needs.

Non-striving. Have you ever felt like you're spending your whole life moving from one external goal to the next? Mindfulness offers another approach. Non-striving is a practice of engaging in the process rather than the outcome. The principle of non-striving in mindfulness encourages you to become aware of the sources of your motivations and to make the choice to respond to internal motivations rather than external rewards and pressures. Non-striving allows enjoyment of an activity for its own sake, to seeing the value of fully "being" in your experiences.

Letting go. It's easy to form attachments to ideas, ways of being, or relationships that are familiar, including those with negative impacts on us. Even your relationship with mindfulness could turn into an unhealthy attachment: *I have to meditate at least 30 minutes a day every single day, or I'm a failure!* Letting go frees you from clinging to ideas, ways of being, or relationships that no longer serve you.

Mindfully Managing Depression

Doesn't it feel like our society is way too rushed, always encouraging us to manage multiple tasks at once? With so much societal encouragement to keep *doing*, it can be hard to slow down. When we feel the pressure to always keep going, we can end up overriding our natural need to take time for rest and repair. The more we ignore our emotional and physical cues for rest and recuperation, the more likely we are to suffer from burnout, chronic illness, and depression.

Unfortunately, depression is not something you can *think* yourself out of. If it were, there wouldn't be so many intelligent and creative people suffering from it. It's important to understand that being depressed isn't a problem that can be "fixed" or "solved." In fact, the very act of trying to "fix" depression can pull you further down its slippery slope. Many people with depression try to cope by seeking to avoid, change, or ignore how they feel, which often leads to shame, isolation, and feeling worse. If you've tried going that route, don't be hard on yourself for it. When you're struggling with depression, you can often feel like you're on autopilot—stuck in how bad you feel with an urgency to *just feel better.* But there are mindfulness tools that when regularly used can lead to long-term recovery.

Depression is a condition that can be successfully managed using mindfulness principles. The mindful approach is to create healthy distance from negative thoughts, feelings, and behaviors instead of ignoring or avoiding them. By enhancing self-awareness, flexibility, and distress tolerance, you can improve your ability to focus and regulate your emotional states. You have the power to choose how you respond in order to take better care of yourself and prevent depression from taking control of your life.

How Mindfulness Can Help

Sometimes when we're depressed, well-meaning people suggest that a simple shift in perspective will solve our problems. But trying to think positive, happy thoughts can't eliminate depression any more than going for a run can sweat out a case of the flu.

Rather than a quick fix, mindfulness is a practical life skill that can help you address some of the underlying causes of depression by helping you slow down your mind and attune to your body. Doing that allows you to notice, without judgment, the thoughts, feelings, and beliefs that keep you stuck in habitual ways of thinking and feeling. The exercises in this book aren't intended as a cure-all for every one of your day-to-day struggles. You may still have hard days. However, as you learn to apply the principles of mindfulness, you'll find yourself approaching old situations in new ways with new tools at your disposal. This workbook offers a combination of exercises, reflections, and meditations to help you feel more prepared to manage those difficult days. My hope is that with these skills, you'll be able to experience relief, develop resilience, and gain clarity so you can live the life you want, free from depression.

> Mindfulness is a practical life skill that can help you address some of the underlying causes of depression by helping you slow down your mind and attune to your body.

Depression Is Not Just a State of Mind

It's estimated that 16.2 million adults in the United States have a major depressive episode each year.

And even though the field of mental health has made great strides in addressing this too-common condition, many in the general public still believe that depression is a personal failing, as a case of being overly emotional or not trying hard enough to make themselves feel better. Here are some truths that may help you in discussing your condition with friends or family or advancing your own understanding of depression.

Depression is an illness. The medical community recognizes depression as a condition that can be diagnosed and treated; it's not a personal failing or weakness. According to the American Psychiatric Association, depression is defined as a common medical illness that negatively affects how you feel, the way you think, and how you act. Depression can cause feelings of sadness and loss of interest in activities once enjoyed. It can lead to emotional and physical problems and decrease a person's ability to function at work or at home.

Depression is different for everyone. Depression is not a one-size-fits-all diagnosis. For some, the experience is what we might expect: bouts of sadness, difficulty getting out of bed in the morning, and a lack of interest in the things we used to enjoy. In other cases, depression could be marked with stomachaches, sleeping too much or too little, and distancing oneself from loved ones. Your own experience of depression might include all or none of these things. The way depression affects each of us is influenced by our genetics, life experiences, and the resources available to us. Similarly, people develop depression for many different reasons. Many people with depression feel alone in their suffering, isolated by judgmental thoughts like *Why am I feeling bad when nothing is really wrong?* or *There are others who have it worse than I do.* Feeling alone in your struggles can make it hard to talk about them. But keep in mind that you're not alone—millions of people are affected by depression.

Depression can be complex. Ongoing developments in mind–body medicine help us understand how depression impacts us mentally and physically. You may have heard that depression is just the result of bad genetics or not enough feel-good chemicals in our nervous system. But the totality of research suggests that depression is the result of a dynamic combination of factors that includes genetics, the environment you grew up in, life stressors, how you manage stress, and how your body reacts to stressors. Some of us may be predisposed to depression; others may develop it in response to grief, their environment, or difficult changes in their lives.

We can think of depression a result of our biology interacting with external factors. Things change in life, hard things happen, and depression is one way that our body and mind respond to difficult times. It makes sense that a painful event would trigger a period of time when we sleep a lot, eat more, and want to spend the majority of our time alone—this is an extreme version of rest, after all. But in some people, this reaction may be a sign of depression, which inhibits our ability to live the life we want or enjoy the life we have.

As interesting as all that may be, knowing the mechanism behind your depression isn't necessary for recovery. In this book, we'll focus less on the causes of your depression and more on how to manage your condition. You'll learn how mindfulness can help you tune into your different emotional states and prevent a downward spiral of negative self-talk and judgments that keeps you feeling low. No matter the root of your specific experience of depression—trauma, seasonal changes, difficult life events—this workbook will give you the resources to manage both your good days and hard days.

Thoughts and Beliefs

Depression alters how you view the world. The way we cope with life's challenges can be a by-product of our personal experiences and our *belief system*, which can be thought of as a pair of glasses that filters how we see, internalize, and think about our experiences. When you're struggling with depression, having a low mood can influence that filter, tinting your thoughts in a negative way. People struggling with depression can have a very hard time making changes that could potentially help them feel better because their thinking is so negatively skewed. It becomes difficult to see new solutions to old problems.

That said, it's important not to get caught up in the idea that the way to handle this is to avoid negative thoughts—to do whatever it takes to eliminate them. For one thing, avoiding negative thoughts is, at best, a short-term solution because it's so difficult a strategy to maintain. Secondly, negative thoughts are simply one aspect of depression. Stopping them will only get you so far; you'll have to address the underlying issues that influence negative thinking patterns. Otherwise, they'll return again and again.

Emotional Patterns

Like our thoughts and beliefs, our emotions also have a way of coloring our view of the world. We've all received messages throughout our lives about our feelings and how to make sense of them. You may have had help learning how to understand and manage your emotions, or you may still be learning. When we're struggling with depression, what ability we have to manage our emotions can go out the window as we become desperate for anything that might make us feel better—even if it's only for a short amount of time. Short-term solutions may feel good in the moment, but we can't avoid our emotions or distract ourselves from them forever. Mindfulness can help you understand, accept, and work with your feelings, allowing for a deeper, more sustainable recovery from depression.

Stress and Trauma

Most of us would agree that stress and trauma are painful. In this fast-paced world we live in, stress is hard to avoid. Many little things can happen in an ordinary day that cause us stress: reading the news, arguing with a friend, getting stuck in traffic. When we're stressed, it can be easy to focus on our thoughts and miss what's happening in our body, tiring ourselves out because we don't listen to our bodies' cues to rest. Over time, stress can accumulate and impact our emotional health as well, which can sometimes lead to depression. Trauma is an extreme version of stress—typically the result of a significant painful event in our lives. Traumatic experiences and chronic stress can impact our capacity to be aware of what's happening in the present moment, all of which can contribute to depression.

TREATMENT

Because depression impacts so many areas of life, many people find that their recovery needs to be multifaceted. That is, treating depression effectively often requires integration of multiple recovery tools and practices.

This workbook isn't meant to serve as therapy, a diagnostic tool, or anything other than an adjunct support to treatment you're already receiving. If you've come to this book without an existing treatment plan, know that if depressive symptoms are interfering with your ability to function or you're experiencing thoughts of suicide or self-harm, it's wise to consult a healthcare professional. Help is available—see the resource list at the back of this book (page 155). With proper diagnosis and treatment, you can overcome depression and experience relief.

How to Use This Workbook

In the following chapters, you'll learn and practice many techniques that will show you how to apply mindfulness to help reduce the severity and duration of your depressive episodes. Each chapter explores one of the core mindfulness principles: beginner's mind, non-judgment, acceptance, patience, trust, non-striving, and letting go. In each chapter you'll find varied exercises, from simple meditations to visualizations to journaled reflections to self-care activities. There may be exercises in this workbook that do not resonate with your needs. I encourage you to move on after giving them a chance and to consider returning to them at some point.

Allow yourself to move through the chapters in whatever order makes sense to you. Focus on the areas that will help you integrate mindfulness into your daily life. Remember, you're the expert on what you need the most. This workbook is meant to serve as a support, whatever that means for you—there is no wrong way to use it.

Before You Begin

Congratulations! You've taken an important step toward feeling better. By picking up this workbook, you've demonstrated that you're open to investing time and effort into taking care of yourself. As you move forward, keep these points in mind:

Mindfulness is a process. It's not a destination, it's a journey, and you're in charge of the expedition. You may find yourself doing exercises back-to-back; you might decide to rely on a few particularly helpful practices, and you might have days where you skip doing any exercise entirely. Allow yourself to approach mindfulness in ways that fit with your lifestyle and preferences.

Sometimes the process is uncomfortable. Mindfulness is an introspective practice that helps us gain self-awareness. Learning more about ourselves can bring up some painful feelings, especially if depression has kept you from addressing them. It's important to honor yourself, go slowly, and take time to be with your experience. Don't forget to be patient with yourself (a principle of mindfulness discussed in chapter 5, page 73).

Show yourself compassion. The most important aspect of mindfulness is self-compassion. Working on these exercises is not about how quickly you can complete the workbook; progress comes from really engaging with the materials and exercises so you can integrate them into your daily life. It may be helpful to set a schedule for yourself; for example, decide to spend 5 to 10 minutes every other day working on the exercises. But beware of slipping into all-or-nothing thinking patterns, such as *I have to use this workbook every day* or *If I don't keep to the schedule, I'm a failure.* Consistency is key and helps build healthy, sustainable habits. But life happens, so if your progress is interrupted, don't be hard on yourself, and don't berate yourself. Be gentle with yourself, and just pick back up again when you're able.

NOTES ABOUT EXERCISES

In general, the exercises in this book will be more beneficial if practiced and reflected on more than once. You may notice that you learn something different about yourself each time. Decide for yourself which are most helpful and how often to use them. Each chapter's selection of exercises will begin with a simple grounding meditation that's especially easy to do and helpful whenever you're feeling stressed or distracted.

Most of these activities work best if performed in a safe, comfortable, quiet space—a place where you won't be interrupted or distracted. (Remember to turn off your phone or put it on mute.) For some people, this may be a bedroom or den. For others, it could be outdoors in a favorite spot. It depends on what feels comfortable for you in the moment you're doing your practice.

Some exercises invite you to close your eyes, but if you prefer to keep them open, just relax the muscles around your eyes and let your vision soften. If your depression is related to significant trauma and during your mindfulness practice you experience a flashback or begin to panic, it's important to pause the meditation and examine ways to help calm your body in the moment. Some options include calling a friend to help ground you; switching to a coping activity that can help to calm your brain, such as coloring, journaling, or listening to music; or engaging in some physical exercise, like walking or yoga. Overall, it's important to listen to your body if flashbacks and panic occur. If these continue to occur, consult with a mental health professional to better understand why they are happening.

CHAPTER TWO

BEGINNER'S MIND

Starting something new isn't always easy. And yet it can be refreshing to begin a new venture with no preconceived ideas about how things will go or what the experience should look like. Imagine getting ready for a trip to a new, unknown place. When your excitement outweighs any anxieties about the unknowns and the unexpected, you stay open to new experiences. Beginner's mind emulates this attitude of being open to every possibility. In this chapter, you'll explore your beginner's mind by noticing when you feel open to the new and when you start to feel closed or caught up in old story lines.

The Mindful Way

Many people who struggle with depression develop habituated ways of react-ing, patterns of negative thinking that inadvertently become an ingrained habit. To some degree, we all do this; we all have experiences that inform how we view the world and how we respond. But over time, relying too much on habitual reactions can weaken our ability to see things in a fresh way. That's where the mindfulness principle of beginner's mind comes in. Beginner's mind is a way of being that encourages openness, receptivity, and hope, the qualities of approaching something for the first time. When we get caught up in responding to new situations in old ways, we can practice the principle of beginner's mind by first noticing our reactions, taking a breath, and then choosing to do something different.

When you're burdened by depression, it can be easy to always see the glass as half-empty, when in reality it's also half-full. Beginner's mind can help shift your perspective and help you practice looking at the whole glass. Beginner's mind allows you to have a childlike sense of wonder, a natural flow of curiosity and openness to new experiences. It includes eagerness, excitement, and connection to a natural state of play and exploration. When practicing beginner's mind, the response to a half glass of water could be *look how pretty the light looks in the glass*.

Though you can explore the principles of mindfulness in any order, beginner's mind is particularly helpful at the start of your mindfulness prac-tice. When you're first practicing mindfulness to manage your depression, the experience may sometimes feel uncomfortable. As you learn to notice depression-related negative thoughts and feelings that you've tried to avoid, you might feel some distress. Beginner's mind can help you keep going as you learn the other principles of mindfulness.

Common Mental and Emotional Patterns

Depression might be considered the nemesis of beginner's mind. We could even call depression "stale mind," a recurring been-there-done-that belief that nothing will work. When you're trapped in stale mind, it can be difficult to remember that every moment can be approached with a fresh point of view. During a particularly long winter, it's hard to remember that spring eventually comes back with the freshness of new life.

Most of us have a hard time trying something new, especially something that may challenge the way we're used to living our lives. Depression has a way of filtering our outlook, making it very tempting to buy into the self-doubting thoughts that arise when we enter a new experience:

I don't know if I can do this.

I don't know how to do it right.

I don't have time.

I don't think this will work.

These negative thoughts may seem benign, but they have a way of building up over time. In this chapter, we'll explore some methods for developing a beginner's mindset so you can grow your mindfulness practice and welcome new experiences in your life.

SOMETHING DIFFERENT

Jenny, a bright, creative, 34-year-old project manager, came into my office seeking relief from depression. A self-proclaimed perfectionist, Jenny suffered from nagging self-doubt and a chronic sense of emptiness. For months, she'd been feeling anxious that she wasn't doing her best at work and would spend many hours a day thinking about what she "should" be doing better. Jenny began spending more time at the office; she'd come home exhausted and then sit in front of the TV until she passed out on the couch. She spent less and less time with friends and loved ones, and by the time Jenny started therapy, she had little contact with anyone outside of her job. During her first sessions, Jenny was very skeptical of how mindfulness would help her. I asked, "What would be so bad about trying something different? If it doesn't work, you can continue doing what you've been doing." She agreed to try.

Jenny began to implement breathing exercises into her daily practice. She reported an understanding of how much she'd been pushing away her feelings. She began to gain more self-awareness, realizing that she hadn't been leaving herself time to do what she enjoys—instead, she'd allowed negative feedback at work to override her self-care, leading to burnout. Jenny was able to feel sad about how disconnected from her friends she'd become and began to reach out to make plans with them. Approaching her situation with a beginner's mind enabled Jenny to become less judgmental and more self-compassionate and recognize the areas where she needed to explore and grow.

Simple Meditation

The exercise set in each chapter will begin with a *grounding exercise*. Whenever you're feeling overwhelmed by stress or overloaded with emotions, implementing a grounding exercise is a great way to reset and self-soothe.

Beginner's mind is the fertile soil where you can grow your mindfulness practice. Grounding exercises are particularly helpful as a first step to enter into a beginner's mind. As we grow into adulthood, we are often pressured to ignore our need to be soothed and calmed in the service of being productive and efficient. The sense of childlike wonder that defines beginner's mind starts with grounding exercises because feeling secure and safe is a necessary foundation for playfulness and exploration.

This exercise utilizes *sensory grounding*, the practice of coming fully into your experience by connecting with the wide range of the sensory stimuli available to you. There are many ways to ground yourself using the senses; this exercise works by prompting you to notice and take in the details of your surroundings using each of your senses in turn. It's called the 5-4-3-2-1 technique.

To begin, find a comfortable position in a quiet place where you won't be disturbed.

Answer each of the following questions. Feel free to answer out loud or in your head if you don't have writing materials available.

What are 5 things you can see?

What are 4 things you can touch?

What are 3 things you can hear?

What are 2 things you can smell?

What is 1 thing you can taste?

After completing the exercise, relax in place for a few minutes, bringing your attention to the sensations of your body.

Deep Breathing Balloon

Because of unaddressed stress and tension, many people with depression unknowingly have poor posture or constricted movements that limit their ability to take a deep, refreshing, oxygenated breath. Abdomen breathing is a deep breathing technique that helps you get into the habit of expansive breathing from the base of your lungs, which can help you move toward a more open, receptive, and curious mindset that supports beginner's mind. Deep abdomen breathing can also lower blood pressure and slow the heartbeat, helping oxygen-rich blood circulate throughout your body. Conversely, shallow breathing can shift your nervous system into a fight/flight/freeze mode, which may contribute to negative thoughts and emotional distress.

Exploring something as mundane as breathing in an exercise like this is a way to start expanding into your beginner's mind. When you're experiencing a new way of breathing, you're making space for something different to happen.

To start, find a comfortable position, sitting with your hands in your lap or lying down on your back.

1. Note how stressed you feel right now using the scale provided.

0	1	2	3	4	5
not stressed					extremely stressed

2. Close your eyes and imagine your stomach as a balloon.

3. Take a deep breath in through your nose and count to five, pushing your breath all the way down to your stomach, allowing your balloon to fully expand as you inhale.

4. Once you've filled your balloon, hold your breath as you count to three.

5. Slowly exhale through your nose, counting to seven as you fully deflate your balloon.

6. Now rate your stress level again.

0	1	2	3	4	5
not stressed					extremely stressed

Repeat the breathing exercise until you reach your desired number on the scale. You don't have to get to 1 or 0 for the exercise to be success-ful; what matters is lowering your stress to a level that's manageable for you in the moment. This exercise can be practiced daily as a way to create a new habit of breathing. It can also be used during times when you feel stressed, anxious, or depressed.

Hungry Monk

In this exercise, you'll practice beginner's mind by experiencing something familiar as if you were experiencing it for the first time. When we're burdened by depression, it's easy to go through our daily routines mindlessly. Consider the last meal you ate: By the end of it, you might barely remember what you had or what it tasted like or whether you felt full. When we apply mindfulness to the way we eat, our beginner's mind transforms this mundane activity into a soothing, grounding experience.

For this exercise, choose a food that's delightful but simple. Many people enjoy doing this exercise with a piece of chocolate, some raisins, or a small cracker. Once the exercise comes easier to you, you can cultivate your beginner's mind further by expanding the practice to include entire meals.

1. Hold your food item between your thumb and index finger.

2. Imagine that you're a small child and this is the first time you've ever held this food.

3. Notice what reactions are happening in your mouth, stomach, and hands as you see and feel this object.

4. Bring the food to your nose and inhale. Notice the aromas wafting into your nostrils.

5. Observe whatever feelings arise as you perceive the odors of the food.

6. Lower the food item, taking care to notice any thoughts that may be coming to mind.

7. Allow yourself to continue holding the food, feeling its texture, and observing its colors and shape.

8. When you feel ready, bring the food item to your lips, and take a bite or place the item in your mouth.

9. Allow yourself to chew slowly. Notice the taste of your food item, the sensation of it dissolving in your mouth, the textures against your tongue and teeth. How many different flavors can you detect? What does it feel like as you chew? Take note of any thoughts that come to mind.

10. A few moments after you're done chewing, allow yourself to notice your reactions and feelings. Record your observations in the space provided:

What thoughts are coming to your mind?

....

....

....

....

What feelings are you experiencing?

....

....

....

....

What sensations are happening in your body?

Sharing is Caring

Sometimes depression makes it difficult to think about things we love and things that bring us pleasure without also feeling complicated negative feelings like loss, disappointment, and failure. This exercise takes us out of depression-related negative associations by focusing our attention on the pleasant, loving feelings we have for something or someone outside ourselves. In this activity, you'll work on allowing yourself to experience positive emotions without fear of losing them by generously sharing the feelings with others. This heartfelt generosity is unfettered, like beginner's mind.

This is a drawing exercise, but don't be concerned about your skill level or how "good" the drawings are. The purpose is reflective expression, not getting attached to a particular outcome. If you prefer to use words instead of images, go ahead! Try to take a playful, non-judgmental approach, like a child drawing pictures just for the fun of it.

Take a piece of paper, whatever type is available to you, and lay it horizontally on your table, desk, or drawing surface. Divide the page into four columns, numbered from one to four.

Consider using crayons, colored pencils, or markers for your drawings. Take your time and be mindful of your senses as you create. How do your art supplies feel in your hand? What colors, scents, and sounds are present as you draw? Take note of any thoughts that arise as you're working, but try your best to not allow them to interrupt your work.

In column one, draw a place where you love to be. It could be indoors or outdoors, a place you go to often, or a place from your memory. Include whatever details are important to you, but don't fixate on making an accurate or realistic image. Create something that's meaningful to you.

In column two, draw a picture of an activity you love doing. You can put yourself in the picture or just depict objects or actions that represent the activity to you.

In column three, draw a picture of someone you love to spend time with. This doesn't need to be a person! It could be a pet, the birds that frequent your backyard birdfeeder, or any presence whose company you enjoy.

In column four, draw a picture of a person or a place you would want to send your love to.

After you're done with your drawings, turn the page over. Write down whatever thoughts and feelings you're experiencing, and try to keep writing until the page is full.

ENCOURAGING WORDS

As you work through these exercises, don't forget to show yourself some appreciation and celebrate small victories! You've picked up this book today, and now you're reading this page; that's a success and move toward feeling better. Remember, the most rewarding journeys begin with a single step. Even if you go no further today, it just means you've put down the book for now and can start again tomorrow.

Embracing Difficult Feelings

Have you noticed that children and animals seem to shake off negative feelings more easily than adults? What would happen if you didn't avoid uncomfortable feelings and instead tried to embrace them? Such a radical approach requires a beginner's mind.

This exercise is a way of responding with pure compassion and acceptance to your difficult feelings, the way one child instinctively offers a hug to another child who's upset. When you bring your attention, compassion, and understanding to feelings such as sadness and fear, you're embracing a growth opportunity. You use your beginner's mind to handle hard emotions with the ease and innocence of childlike compassion.

Take 5 to 10 minutes to complete this exercise, more time if you need it or less if you want to stop sooner.

1. Find a comfortable position, sitting with your hands in your lap or lying down on your back.

2. Call to mind a situation that is or has been difficult for you to go through. It can be something of low to moderate level of difficulty; you may want to start with a low level when practicing this for the first time.

3. Notice any feelings of discomfort. Recognize any thoughts or impulses to move away from these feelings (wanting to make a call, needing to check your phone, wanting to eat a snack, worrying about your to-do list).

4. Breathe deeply through your nose and exhale slowly through your mouth for two or three breaths.

5. Imagine a loving or compassionate person in your life, now or from the past. Imagine this person saying kind words or giving you a warm, loving hug.

6. When you perceive a calm and loving feeling in your mind and body, turn your attention back to the difficult situation and feelings you were trying to move away from.

7. Let the difficult feeling know you are paying attention. Imagine embracing the difficult feeling with the compassion and kindness that you felt earlier.

8. Offer loving statements such as "I'm here with you—it will be okay" as many times as you need until you feel your mind and body relax and calm down.

This exercise can be helpful to use before or after situations that activate difficult feelings or thoughts. It can also be used as a daily ritual in the morning or evening to build tolerance to negative emotions and strengthen emotional flexibility and resilience.

Mindful Breathing

This exercise will teach you to integrate mind and body by using your breath to slow down your thoughts. We spend most of our lives not very aware of how we're breathing. But how our breath moves through our body can say a lot about our mental state. For example, when we breathe from the abdomen (see exercise 1, page 19), we tend to feel more relaxed and present. When we breathe from our chest, we tend to feel more anxious and disconnected from what's happening in the present.

It can be challenging the first time you try to focus on your breath because you'll likely become more aware of your thoughts. When you finish the exercise, you can explore those thoughts.

1. Find yourself a comfortable position, sitting or lying down.

2. Close your eyes, or softly focus on an object or spot in front of you.

3. Bring awareness to your breathing. Feel the sensations of your breath moving in and out as you inhale and exhale. Let your breathing settle into a slow, comfortable pace.

4. As you inhale, imagine air slowly filling a balloon in your stomach. Let the balloon inflate completely.

5. As you exhale, imagine the balloon slowly deflating.

6. Continue breathing steadily. Notice your stomach moving in and out as you inflate and deflate your balloon.

7. When you notice your mind wandering, gently tell the distracting thought, *There you are. I'll be right with you when I'm finished.* Then direct your attention to the sensations of breathing, allowing your focus to return the balloon in your stomach, slowly filling as you inhale and slowly deflating as you exhale

8. Continue the exercise for a couple of minutes.

When you're finished, open your eyes or let go of any focus, and allow your mind to relax. Take a moment to look around to orient yourself. Notice the colors, textures, lighting, and temperature of your surroundings. Notice your thoughts, how your body feels, and any emotions you may be experiencing.

Choose one thought that you had during or after the exercise, and answer the questions in the space provided.

What thoughts did you notice the most while you were breathing?

On a scale of 1 to 5 (1 = very easy, 5 = very hard), how easy was it to reassure yourself when your mind wandered and return your attention back to your breathing?

What helped bring attention back to your breath?

Did you notice anything happening in your body when your attention came back to your breath? For example, did you feel tension or relaxation?

How are you feeling now?

During the exercise, you reassured yourself that any thoughts that came up would be addressed later. Take some time now to write down any thoughts that may need further time and attention.

Mindful Moment: Beginner's Mind

When you're depressed, it's especially hard to gain perspective. It's like going through many cold rainy days and feeling like the sun will never come out. Depression can put a damper on the way we think, feel, and act, making it really easy to believe that everything will always happen the way it did before. To make matters even worse, this mindset prompts us to avoid the very acts that will help us see things differently. Convinced that our story will never change, we stop trying. We stagnate, and over time this stale point of view leads to more negative feelings and more depression.

Where depression limits flexibility and narrows the way we think, beginner's mind brings expansion and increases our capabilities. When you use the principle of beginner's mind, you're questioning the old, worn paths that your mind usually travels. When you take a moment to create space for a new point of view on an old experience, you're blazing a fresh path that may lead to other undiscovered thoughts and feelings. The more we learn to be open to possibilities, take in simple pleasures, and approach each experience with the freshness of a beginner's mind, the less power the old story lines and depression-related preoccupations have over us.

Change doesn't just happen out of the blue; it takes work. And when you're living with depression, the internal resources you can use to navigate change are limited. When you feel that change will never come or isn't coming fast enough, call on your beginner's mind to loosen your fixation on how things should be, and take on a fresh and open attitude that allows for all types of possibilities. When you're having doubts, your beginner's mind can remind you that you can always go back to what you know, so what's the harm in trying something new? To risk being curious, take things one breath at a time, and reflect on what you notice along the way . . . these may seem like small steps. But in no time, they may lead you to new, unknown experiences yet to be discovered. The joy of beginner's mind is this freedom to wonder. It can be one of the most liberating practices, helping to free you from the constraints of depressive thinking.

AFFIRMATION

Each chapter will end with an affirmation, a short and simple positive phrase that you can recite and repeat whenever you need some positivity. This chapter's affirmation is to remind you that sometimes change happens over time:

I am learning and growing every day.

You can start your day with an affirmation to begin in a fresh way and set a positive tone. Or call to mind a positive affirmation to counter your negative thoughts when you're in a situation that will bring up difficult feelings or self-criticism. An affirmation can also be used as a pep talk while getting dressed, taking a shower, preparing for a meeting, or anytime you need it.

CHAPTER TAKEAWAYS

1. Beginner's mind is the feeling we have when we start something new without a preconception about how it should go. It's a feeling of curiosity, wonder, hope, and openness to every possibility.

2. Depression is in some ways the opposite of beginner's mind because it creates a mindset that nothing can change or get better.

3. Grounding exercises are helpful for encouraging beginner's mind and help us rest and self-soothe.

4. Beginner's mind is useful for starting a mindfulness practice.

5. We can use our breath to connect mind and body, by focusing attention on our breathing and giving us the space to consider our difficult thoughts and feelings from a fresh point of view.

The Mindfulness Workbook for Depression

CHAPTER THREE

NON-JUDGMENT

Judging ourselves has a funny way of keeping us isolated. Often, we judge ourselves harshly as a way of trying to feel okay: We assume that others will be hard on us, so we try to preempt the anticipated judgment by quickly attacking ourselves for our imagined imperfections. We tell ourselves, *The tougher I am on myself, the safer I am with others because they aren't as likely to be as hard on me as I am on myself.* Better the devil we know—our own critical voice—than unexpected judgment from other people. But instead of feeling safer, we end up feeling more lonely and stagnant. That's because our self-judgments take the place of actual interactions that reveal people's true thoughts and feelings toward us. They keep us from being open to hearing all the ways people feel toward us, including the positive thoughts and feelings. Practicing the mindfulness principle of non-judgment instead helps us become available to connect with others and to handle whatever comes up in the interaction.

The Mindful Way

When we're struggling with depression, it can be easy to get caught up in thinking about everything that we're *not* doing. Even without depression, negative thoughts in general are cyclical and persistent; the more we focus on what we don't want, the more we notice the negatives in our lives. This is true for everyone because human beings are hardwired for *negativity bias.* Our instinct to pay extra attention to potential dangers has ensured the survival of our species, keeping us away from risky situations and motivating us to prepare for the worst. According to leading negativity bias researcher psychologist Rick Hanson, "In the tough environments where our ancestors lived—if they missed a carrot, they usually had a shot at another one later on. But if they failed to avoid a [hazard]—WHAM, no more chances to pass on their genes."

Negativity bias is part of our ingrained behavior, a precaution to keep us from getting hurt. But this survival reflex can go too far if left unchecked. And depression's impact on our mindset, as discussed in the previous chapter, makes it all too easy to surrender to negativity. When you're depressed, you can build a habit of always giving in to your negativity bias, relying solely on its judgment when thinking about yourself and others. The practice of mindfulness seeks to mediate our negativity bias by orienting our minds to pay attention to our positive experiences. According to researchers at Greater Good Science Center at the University of California, Berkeley, mindfulness helps us break free from negativity because of two key components:

1. Mindfulness helps us maintain focus and attention on our thoughts and feelings.

2. Mindfulness helps us accept our thoughts and feelings without judgment.

So let's turn again to the example of a glass of water: Is it half-empty or half-full? If you're looking with negativity bias, you'll see it as half-empty, and you may worry that you're going to run out of water before your thirst is quenched. The mindful way would have us notice our thoughts and feelings in this moment and then acknowledge the water in the glass simply as water in a glass.

In everyday life, we can find ourselves trapped in negativity bias and not even recognize that we're stuck. There are so many opportunities to judge ourselves: We can be critical of what we wear or what we eat or how much we exercise (or how much we don't). We can get stuck comparing ourselves to others or idealized images of who we would like to be and only seeing the ways that we come up short. The non-judgment principle of mindfulness helps us put negativity bias aside and reminds us that we can only be where we are at this moment. Accepting our experience without judgment, even for just a few moments in our day, can make a big difference. And these small moments of relief can create opportunities for more positive thoughts to take seed and free us from the burden of judgment.

Common Mental and Emotional Patterns

Learning to employ the principle of non-judgment develops your capacity for *discernment*: the ability to know what will serve you and what won't. Discernment is a keen type of perception that helps you see clearer, healthier options. Practicing discernment affords you the feeling of agency or choice.

Depression can cloud your ability to discern what's good for you. It's common for people with depression to struggle with feelings of shame, guilt, and self-critical thoughts. You may judge yourself for those thoughts, blaming yourself for how bad you're feeling: *What's wrong with me? Why do I always feel this bad?* Feelings of hopelessness may lead you to tell yourself, *There are no solutions.* Depression and self-judgment often work in tandem: Sometimes depression can make you more judgmental of yourself, whereas self-judgment can make you feel more depressed.

Non-judgment teaches us to react to those feelings with discernment so we can make a choice to replace negative thoughts with a more helpful way of thinking: *I feel bad; what's going to help me feel better?* Trying out new solutions and replacing self-judgment with discernment allows space for self-compassion and understanding. This helps you stick with what works and walk away from what doesn't so you can continue to develop the resources that help you manage your depression.

JOHNNY'S STORY, PART ONE

Johnny is a 20-year-old college student majoring in political science who struggles with chronic feelings of emptiness, hopelessness, self-doubt, and self-criticism. He was raised by parents who were both lawyers—dinner conversations mostly revolved around competition, academic performance, achievements, and political debates. Little room was left at the table to talk about Johnny's emotional life.

By the time he came to see me, Johnny had high expectations for himself and was very self-critical, rarely meeting his self-imposed expectations. Judgmental thoughts constantly swarmed his mind.

Johnny worked on learning a self-compassion meditation that helped him slow down his breath and focus his attention. When he was in this relaxed and attentive state, he became aware of how judgmental his thoughts were. Over time, he was able to realize that they sounded very familiar, like the reprimands and criticisms he'd heard from his parents growing up. Through practicing discernment, Johnny was able to recognize his self-critical thoughts and replace them with compassionate, self-reflective thoughts. This led to feelings of confidence that allowed him to make more thoughtful choices about how he spent his time. As he deepened his practice of non-judgment, Johnny expanded his toolkit by developing more coping skills, like slowing down to notice his breath, paying attention to his thoughts and feelings, and practicing self-compassion meditations.

Simple Meditation

When you're practicing mindfulness and you learn to pay increased attention to your thoughts, you'll notice many judgmental thoughts that pop up. This grounding exercise helps you notice those negative, judgmental thoughts without engaging and getting distracted by them.

1. Get in a comfortable position, seated or lying down.

2. Close your eyes and bring your awareness to clearing your mind. Take a few slow breaths and focus on the sensations of breathing.

3. Picture yourself sitting by a clear, calm running river with a box of toy sailboats.

4. Continue focusing on your breath. When you have a thought, gently acknowledge the thought by imagining it written on the side of one of your toy sailboats. Say out loud or in your head, *Thank you, thought*. Then imagine placing the sailboat in the river and watching it float downstream.

5. Gently return your attention to your breath. When the next thought arises, repeat these steps: Observe the thought. Thank the thought. Place the thought on a sailboat. Watch it float down the river.

   Continue the meditation for 3 to 10 minutes or longer if you like.

Positive Affirmations

Affirmation meditations are simple but effective for training you to replace the judgmental thought patterns. To create an affirmation, just write down a positive word or thought that describes how you want to feel about yourself. Here are some examples you can use (you'll find others throughout this book):

I am enough.

I am okay just as I am.

I am human, just like everybody else.

To do the meditation, set yourself in a comfortable position with your eyes open or closed, whichever you prefer. Place one hand over your heart and rest the other over your belly. Take a deep breath, imagining the air filling your body and flowing into your hands. Then slowly release your breath and say the affirmation to yourself, out loud, or in your mind.

Notice where your breathing is coming from (your chest? your abdomen?) and notice the level of relaxation in your body.

Repeat the steps as often as you like.

You can do this exercise using any affirmation that's meaningful to you, and you can change the affirmation according to your need.

Self-Compassion Reset

We've all had situations that stir up judgment and critical thoughts about ourselves, leading to feelings of second-guessing or being self-critical. When you're feeling depressed, your ability to be resilient to these self-doubts is compromised even further, leading to extreme self-attacks that activate shame and self-loathing. Self-compassion exercises like this one are essential in strengthening your ability to tolerate these judgmental blows, bringing you more understanding and compassion and decreasing shame. This exercise can be used anytime you notice moments of stress, negativity, or discomfort.

To start, think of an event that's activated a negative thought or judgment about yourself. Notice if you can feel the distress it causes in your body. Then follow these steps:

1. Bring your awareness to the place of tension. Note it with your thoughts, and if possible place your hand on the tense area.

2. Say in your mind: *I feel compassion for my pain.*

3. Say in your mind: *I have all I need within me to face this.*

4. Say in your mind: *I accept all feelings, the good and the bad.*

5. Imagine sending compassion from your heart to all the parts of your body that hold tension.

Notice what happens to the tension and self-judgmental thoughts. Write down any thoughts or feelings that arose or changed during the exercise.

Positivity Bias

The principle of non-judgment applies to all areas of our life, including in our relationships with ourselves and with others. When someone or something outside our control causes us distress, it can be hard to take a mindful moment before reacting with negativity bias and judgment. When we're feeling down about ourselves—a frequent consequence of depression—we tend to make more snap judgments about others. Our negativity bias brings prior bad experiences to mind, so we assume the worst about someone to decrease our risk of being hurt. And this short-term reaction shuts off our ability to stay connected with others and learn more about ourselves and about them.

This exercise helps you map out your thoughts and feelings, increasing your understanding and connection to your own feelings and helping shift away from negativity bias into a positive direction.

To start, think of a recent or past upsetting event that activated a negative bias or judgment on your part toward someone or something outside you. As you recollect, notice any distress it causes in your body. Next, fill in the columns provided.

In the first column, write down a judgmental thought you had during the incident.

Examples: *What a weird comment. He's a mean person.*

In the second column, identify the feeling that came with the thought.

Examples: *fear, sadness, irritation*

In the third column, write down a thought that shows positive bias, providing a valid, compassionate way of viewing the situation.

Examples: *That's a unique point of view. I didn't think of that.* Or, *He seems really unhappy. He must be going through something.*

Negative Bias	Feeling	Positive Bias

Negative Bias	Feeling	Positive Bias

Afterward, take a moment to reflect on the exercise. What did you notice while you were engaging in the exercise? Were there any thoughts or feelings that surprised you? Remember that negativity bias is a natural survival instinct; by identifying your negative thoughts as a point of view that can be shifted, you may begin to notice a change in your attitude and perspective.

Try this exercise at the end of each day or at the end of a workweek to reflect and observe your thoughts or biases without getting caught up in a judgmental story line. See if this prevents you from carrying a narrative over to the following day or week.

ENCOURAGING WORDS

Chances are that as you work your way through this book, you're paying a lot more attention to your thoughts, feelings, and breath than you normally do. Like going back to the gym after a long break, you may sometimes feel tired and out of practice. However, being tired is a sign that you're getting good exercise and building up your internal and external resources. Keep up the good work, and keep moving forward!

Self-Compassion Ritual

Rituals are important and effective for building lasting, meaningful changes in our lives. You may think habits and rituals are interchangeable, but the two couldn't be more different. A habit is a mostly unconscious behavior, whereas a ritual involves intentional, purposeful, and meaningful action. Rituals can help us take ownership of and give direction to our behaviors . . . and eventually lead to healthy habits.

The antidote to judgment is compassion. Cultivating compassion infuses a gentle, friendly awareness to any situation where you're tempted to judge yourself. This exercise is designed to help you develop a self-compassion ritual, building the healthy habit of sending compassion toward yourself and others. Rituals that include caring for yourself and others may help bolster self-esteem and gentleness in the face of judgment and harsh criticisms. Like a good friend who has your back during difficult times, you can kindly give yourself space and reassurance. Try practicing this for 3 to 10 minutes at least once or twice a week to build and strengthen your compassion muscles.

1. Set a timer for the length of the ritual. Sit comfortably and notice your breathing. Spend some time feeling the sensations of your breath, relaxing into a comfortable rhythm.

2. Place your hand over your heart and say, *I accept all my feelings and thoughts. I am okay just as I am.*

3. Focus on a mildly judgmental thought you have toward something. It can be about yourself, another person, or a situation. Keep the object of your thought at the forefront of your mind.

4. When you start becoming aware of the judgment and negativity that accompany the object of your thoughts, hold your hand over your heart and say to yourself, the imagined person, or the situation: *I am sending compassion and acceptance. I appreciate you. I see you and hear you.*

5. Breathe steadily and focus on your breathing while continuing to hold your hand over your heart.

6. Repeat to yourself two more times: *I am sending compassion and acceptance. I appreciate you. I see you and hear you.*

7. Pay attention to your breath and your feelings until the ritual time has ended. Notice any thoughts that come up, especially self-judgments. If self-judgments surface, focus your attention on your breathing and any other sensations in your body.

REFLECTION

In the first circle provided, write down one judgmental thought that you had during the ritual.

In these next three circles, write down three compassionate thoughts that you had.

Thank-You Note to Yourself

Gratitude encourages positivity on the part of the giver as well as the receiver. In this exercise, you'll play both roles, putting aside negative bias with a message of gratitude to yourself.

Sit in a comfortable place with writing materials and a cup of tea, coffee, juice, or your favorite relaxing beverage if desired. Set a timer for 5 minutes. In the lines provided or on a separate page, spend the time writing a thank-you note to yourself, not worrying about grammar, spelling, or the perfect words. Just allow any feelings of gratitude that come to your mind to be expressed on the page. If you get distracted or stuck, just notice whatever resistance you have to writing your thoughts. Continue until time runs out.

Mindful Moment: Non-Judgment

I encourage you to notice when you feel the impulse to move away from uncomfortable thoughts and feelings. At those times, pause and consider what you're trying to avoid. Acknowledge whatever feeling you're having without passing judgment on it, and use one of the affirmation statements from this chapter. Non-judgment helps you manage depression by bolstering your self-compassion to help you redirect feelings of self-doubt and negativity bias.

When struggling with depression, you may be so used to being hard on yourself that you don't even realize when you're being self-critical. The mindful practice of non-judgment can help you recognize habitual thought patterns and do something differently. Over time and with some practice, you'll begin to recognize self-judgmental thoughts sooner, note them, and gently set them aside to make room for self-compassion.

Judging isn't something to beat yourself up over. Often it's an attempt at self-protection to preempt potential rejection, embarrassment, and criticisms. It's deeply rooted in our survival instincts as social animals. However, judging also has a way of keeping us isolated by disconnecting us from deeper understanding and well-being. When we judge, we're putting on an armor of protection to separate ourselves from others. The way to calm judgmental thoughts is not to judge ourselves for having them. The practice of self-compassion disrupts our instinctive negativity bias and reminds our survival-motivated brain of the resources and healthy options we have available. Mindfulness is a way to notice judgmental thoughts and gently redirect our energies toward healthier patterns of thinking.

AFFIRMATION

Sometimes when we practice self-compassion, we become more aware of just how hard we're being on ourselves. Here's an affirmation that you might want to try repeating as a reminder to be gentle with yourself:

I accept myself, even when I'm not at my best.

CHAPTER TAKEAWAYS

1. Self-judgment can be used to defend ourselves from hurt, but it may also make us feel more isolated.

2. Negativity bias is our inborn instinct to pay more attention to negative experiences.

3. Non-judgment is the mindfulness principle that helps us notice negative, judgmental thoughts. It makes space for discernment, which is our ability to know which thoughts and feelings are helpful and which aren't.

4. Self-compassion is the antidote to judgment. It helps you become more resilient to self-judgment and criticism.

5. As we become aware of our self-judgment, we can use mindfulness as a tool to replace the judgment with compassion.

CHAPTER FOUR

ACCEPTANCE

At any given moment, we have countless ways to react to what's going on around us. Sometimes we act in ways we're ashamed of, and sometimes we act in ways we're proud of. But at the end of the day, no one is perfect. No one will ever be perfect. The mindfulness principle of acceptance helps us come to understand that we don't need to be anyone but ourselves and teaches us to allow room for our imperfections. When we do that, we can more fully connect with others and, more important, with ourselves. Self-acceptance can help you develop resilience to shame and increase your confidence. It's a key factor in recovering from depression because without self-acceptance, positive interventions can only go so far. You can't take in positive experiences and integrate positive beliefs about yourself if you have difficulty accepting who you are. Practicing acceptance helps you absorb all that mindfulness has to offer.

The Mindful Way

You spend every day with yourself; no matter where you go, you'll always be your own constant companion. Isn't it interesting how we can be our only company, through thick and thin and everything in between, and still not be very nice to ourselves? For most of us, being hard on ourselves is a reflex. We barely notice we're doing it. You might even be doing it now! In chapter 3, we discussed how mindfulness can help with self-judgment and the ways you can begin to notice when you're being harsh with yourself. Once we recognize our self-judgments as simple reactive thoughts, we can come to accept our imperfections instead of passing judgment on them.

When you have negative thoughts about yourself, they trigger a stress response. And for people whose emotional resilience is strained by depression, difficult feelings and experiences become more overwhelming and painful. One of the reasons mindfulness helps people with depression is because it activates the areas in your brain that help you regulate emotions and stress. When you practice self-acceptance, you strengthen your awareness of your thoughts while gently accepting them in the moment, mitigating the likelihood that they will trigger a stress response. This makes the mindful practice of self-acceptance a powerful tool that can improve your ability to tolerate difficult day-to-day experiences.

Common Mental and Emotional Patterns

We can count on certain things to change, like the weather. Seasons come and go, and nature has its rhythms and cycles. There are constants among the uncertainties. Much like the weather, depression has its own cycles and bouts of uncertainty. Through mindfulness, we can become more aware of the moments of hope and beauty that will help us weather the storms of depression.

Instead of *I can't do anything right*, with mindfulness we can tell ourselves, *I'm upset that I can't do this yet, but I'm learning something new.*

Instead of *I shouldn't have said anything—why did I say that?* we can say, *I regret what I said. I wonder how I could have said that differently.*

The preceding replacement statements illustrate the mindfulness principle of acceptance because they validate an authentic feeling while acknowledging that you are a human and make mistakes. Accepting the way you feel as well as your own fallibility offers a more compassionate, growth-oriented attitude toward yourself and others.

JOHNNY'S STORY, PART TWO

In chapter 3 we met Johnny, whose crippling pattern of self-judgment had roots in his childhood, with parents who he felt didn't understand and support him. Being self-critical as a way to motivate himself to do better was the only model Johnny had learned from the way his parents treated him growing up.

As Johnny became aware of the way his judgmental thoughts kept him from understanding what he needed, he was able to accept them as just thoughts. He began to accept that he was different from his academically oriented family—he loved to draw and had a vivid imagination. For him, playing video games and drawing were ways to express his creativity. Doing body scan exercises helped Johnny slow down his thoughts to observe them more clearly and tune into the present. Once he did this, he started noticing the feelings underneath his self-judgment. By using an emotional strength-training writing exercise (like exercise 5 in this chapter), Johnny was able to understand his fears and worries more deeply. He found compassion for how hard he works and allowed himself to grow without pressure to be perfect. The more self-accepting Johnny became, the more he could allow himself to do the things he loved to do—like create art.

Simple Meditation

This three-step grounding exercise is a way to notice your breathing without distractions, doing nothing but being aware of your breath. When you're so busy doing so much in your life, simply noticing your breath can be a way to reset yourself, to be still, and to calm and rest your busy mind.

1. Sit or lie down in a comfortable position. Place one hand just below your throat, on your chest, and place the other hand on your abdomen right above your navel.

2. Close (or partially close) your eyes and spend a minute just breathing. Notice where your breath is coming from. Does your chest or your stomach rise with each inhalation?

3. Allow your breathing to become natural and rhythmic while your mind pays attention to feeling how your hands move as you breathe in and out.

   Continue until you feel calm and still.

Body Scan

This exercise is intended to guide you to notice any thoughts and feelings that accompany your breathing and your body sensations. Practice it regularly to gain acceptance of your physical sensations and a deeper sense of the ways your body can guide and ground your thoughts to the present moment.

1. Start by sitting in a comfortable position with your eyes open or closed—whatever's most comfortable for you.

2. Take a minute to notice your body, feeling the quality of your breathing, your heartbeat, and any tension. Allow yourself to be fully present with whatever you notice.

3. Begin to focus your attention on the top of your head. Note any sensations, from tension, pain, and numbness to warmth, peace, and relaxation.

4. Slowly, at your own pace, move your attention downward. Scan down your neck, then your shoulders, and then the middle of your chest, noting which parts of your body feel relaxed, calm, and peaceful and which parts feel tense, painful, numb, or uncomfortable. Allow yourself to breathe gently, and sense your breath flowing into your entire body as you scan. You may want to visualize a soft, pastel light or coolness pervading your entire body.

5. As your breath goes in and out, notice any thoughts that pull your attention away from being in the present. Acknowledge them without attaching to the thoughts; then gently bring your attention back to your breath and continue scanning.

6. Move your attention through your arms and to the tips of your fingers. Continue scanning and noticing any areas of discomfort or relaxation. Scan down through your stomach, hips, and knees and down to the bottoms of your feet. Move at a pace that's comfortable but not rushed.

7. For the next few minutes or so, pay attention to the parts of your body that feel painful, tense, or numb. Without judgment or agenda, try asking each area what it needs and wants. Gently send acceptance and compassion to that part of your body. If your attention wanders, just bring it back to the uncomfortable, tense parts of your body, and notice without judgment how each body part feels after you spend time giving it attention.

To finish, relax your attention and allow your breath to freely come and go, just as your thoughts do. Let your mind wander in any direction it wants. Gently move your body as you end the exercise.

Attitude of Gratitude

Gratitude is a practice that supports the mindfulness principle of acceptance by helping you shift your focus to what you have instead of what you don't have. Being grateful for your positive qualities creates the strength to welcome other qualities you may have a hard time accepting. Remember, acceptance involves embracing all parts of the self.
In addition, recent studies show that gratitude can help people with depression, stress, and anxiety to feel fewer negative thoughts and more appreciation for the present. This exercise is geared toward helping you actively engage an attitude of gratitude by taking a moment to focus on the things in your life that you are grateful for and appreciate. Fill in your list in the space provided. Give each part as much thought as you like without pressuring yourself to come up with the "best" answer.

Part 1: Myself

List two things about yourself that you appreciate or feel proud of.

_____

_____

Part 2: My life

List two things in your life that you appreciate or feel grateful to have.

_____

_____

Part 3: My circle

Name two people, pets, or role models in your life for whom you're grateful.

....

....

Part 4: My gratitude notes

Write appreciation notes to two people you're grateful for, telling them what you appreciate about them. They can be the same two people from part 3 or two different people. You can also choose to write about a pet or an important memory, expressing your gratitude. These notes are for you to connect with your gratitude and are not necessarily meant to be sent.

....

....

....

....

....

....

....

....

....

Appreciation Walk

Regular exercise has many benefits, including boosting our mood. Many people struggling with depression find that they have a hard time getting themselves moving or become rigid with their exercise routine and don't want to change it. Although there are many health benefits associated with intensive cardiovascular exercise, I recommend including a light walk once a day in whatever exercise regimen you follow. To enhance the mood-boosting benefits on your walk, try adding an appreciation practice by reflecting on your gratitude list from the previous exercise.

Your walk is also an opportunity to employ mindfulness:

Observe and acknowledge the simple wonders that you often take for granted: the temperature of the air on your body, the sounds you encounter, the cracks in the street, and the scents filling your nostrils. Take in the sights, colors, and shapes.

Observe the quality of your thoughts. What experiences do you find enjoyable or not enjoyable? Label these thoughts as thoughts, and let them go.

As you finish, take a moment to pause to reflect on how your body feels. Notice your feet, the sensation of your heart, and the temperature of your hands.

ENCOURAGING WORDS

Art, including the written word, can
be a powerful catalyst to get us in
touch with our feelings. This famous
poem by Robert Frost is a wonderful
metaphor for learning to trust your
intuition and accept the process as you
recover from depression.

THE ROAD NOT TAKEN

Two roads diverged in a yellow wood,
And sorry I could not travel both
And be one traveler, long I stood
And looked down one as far as I could
To where it bent in the undergrowth;

Then took the other, as just as fair,
And having perhaps the better claim,
Because it was grassy and wanted wear;
Though as for that the passing there
Had worn them really about the same,

And both that morning equally lay
In leaves no step had trodden black.
Oh, I kept the first for another day!
Yet knowing how way leads on to way,
I doubted if I should ever come back.

I shall be telling this with a sigh
Somewhere ages and ages hence:
Two roads diverged in a wood, and I—
I took the one less traveled by,
And that has made all the difference.

—ROBERT FROST

Building Emotional Understanding

Building a healthy relationship with ourselves is important for self-acceptance, a major contributor to developing emotional resilience. This exercise is designed to give you an opportunity to have a dialogue with yourself and explore your feelings in a clear way. Emotions can be hard to accept, especially if you don't take the time to understand them better. For most of us, when we don't take the time to understand what is activating our emotions, we have a hard time handling stress and managing our actions, which may lead to lack of self-acceptance and emotional turmoil. This sequence of questions will focus your attention on your emotions; feelings can be hard to accept if you don't take the time to understand them better.

Complete each sentence with the first feeling or thought that comes to your mind. Begin with a behavior you are bothered by or wish were different.

1. I notice I've been acting _____

2. I assume this means I am feeling _____

3. I wonder what is making me feel _____

4. I suspect it is _____

5. I wish I could _____

6. I feel better when I am _____

7. I feel worse when _____

8. I regret when I _____

9. I'm afraid of _____

10. I'm frustrated by _____

11. I'm happier when _____

12. I want _____

13. I appreciate _____

14. I realize _____

15. I hope _____

Emotional Strength Training

In this follow-up to exercise 4, you'll take a closer look at the feelings that you identified and consider their meaning.

1. Choose two statements from the previous exercise that were particularly difficult for you to complete or that you want to understand more deeply.

Example: *I'm afraid of being hurt.*

2. For each of those statements, write a follow-up sentence to explore a possible explanation.

Example: *I'm afraid of being hurt. If I get hurt, I'm afraid I'll never get over it.*

3. Now write an accepting and compassionate response to each of the statements that you explained.

Example: *Of course I'm afraid of getting hurt; getting hurt can feel awful. It's okay to feel scared.*

_____

_____

_____

_____

_____

_____

_____

_____

_____

_____

_____

_____

_____

Mindful Moment: Acceptance

If you think about it, accepting yourself can actually be a lot harder to do than almost anything else.

For one thing, on any given day you're bound to have opportunities to feel bad about yourself in some way. No one does everything perfectly 100 percent of the time. And depression has a way of atrophying our capacity for self-acceptance, making our imperfections seem so much bigger than they are.

The practice of mindfulness is akin to exercising the mental muscles we use to accept ourselves. As we learn to attend to our thoughts and feelings in the present, our potential for self-acceptance grows stronger. It becomes easier to understand that we're all doing the best we can at any given moment or on any given day. Through practicing self-acceptance, you can hold more of your emotions with compassion and build the emotional resilience to help you adjust to the ebbs and flows of life.

One way you can strengthen your self-acceptance muscles is to remind yourself that we all need to take breaks. Pushing harder is not always the answer. And it's okay to take a moment, breathe, and then go back to what you were doing with a fresh mind. The fact that you're reading this book means that there's a part of you that wants to feel better. In my experience, the hardest part of recovery is getting started. And the most important, courageous step is being open to learning and growing. You're already on your journey, so you've demonstrated both qualities! Great work!

AFFIRMATION

Depression can make it easy to slip into feeling anxious and hopeless. Remember, self-acceptance is an ongoing process, and you've taken the first step with this workbook. Take a moment and place a hand on your heart while repeating the following:

I accept myself exactly as I am in this moment.

CHAPTER TAKEAWAYS

1. Self-acceptance can be difficult because depression creates a pattern of critical thoughts that lead to self-doubt.

2. No one is free of mistakes, so we should come to accept our flaws and errors.

3. Self-judgment is stressful; mindfulness exercises our ability to be kind to ourselves and experience self-acceptance instead of self-judgment.

4. Self-acceptance builds internal resources to help you become more resilient to depression-related ebbs and flows.

5. Gratitude to one's self and others is a powerful form of self-acceptance.

The more and more you listen, the more and more you hear; the more and more you hear, the deeper and deeper your understanding becomes.

—DILGO KHYENSTE RINPOCHE
FROM SOGYAL RINPOCHE'S THE TIBETAN BOOK OF LIVING AND DYING

CHAPTER FIVE

PATIENCE

There are so many paths to take in life. It's easy to become pre-occupied with where we want to be instead of being where we are in this moment. The mindfulness principle of patience can help us appreciate the here and now, cultivating a willingness to spend time with whatever our current experience is. Practicing patience is a way of taking care of ourselves; it allows us to take as much time as we need with all of our feelings, both the joyful and the painful.

The Mindful Way

Many of us spend our lives on autopilot, always rushing toward the next milestone. It's an easy mindset to fall into, since we live in an impatient society, always encouraging us to rush toward what lies ahead. We're constantly told that our life will be better on the other side of that weight loss goal, upgraded smartphone, big promotion, or whatever "it" is. This can be exhausting!

In chapter 4, we learned how the mindfulness practice of acceptance can help you become better at understanding and accepting your thoughts, feelings, and experiences. As mindfulness teaches you to notice your self-critical thoughts, acceptance can help you understand that your self-judgments and criticisms are reactions—thoughts that come and go, not truths you need to believe in. The practice of patience gives us the space and support needed to sustain that hard work of accepting our negative thoughts and learning to respond with self-compassion.

Many people struggling with depression find that, over time, noticing and being patient with their thoughts and experiences helps them to be less hard on themselves and more at peace with their experiences, difficult though those experiences can be. Patience tends to help us feel better by cultivating resilience and self-care.

Common Mental and Emotional Patterns

Recovering from depression can be like struggling with a bad cold or flu. If you want to get better, you need to take time to rest and recognize your limits. It's a process, and along the way some days will be easier than others. But every hard day is also an opportunity to notice what you need right here, right now in order to focus on feeling better. Depression forces you to slow down and really focus on what you can and cannot spend energy on.

Depression is like the blinking red light when your phone's battery is low: It's an indication that you need to slow down and use your resources on what really matters. The challenge of depression is that you may want to tend to many things but lack the capacity. When we practice the mindfulness principle of patience, we're giving ourselves permission to just do what we can, not everything we wish we could do. It takes patience to prioritize, taking as much time for ourselves as we need instead of reacting to internal fears or external pressures that demand that we try to do everything.

Instead of *I will never feel better*, try to patiently tell yourself, *I'm feeling a little bit better every day.*

Instead of *I should be feeling better faster*, patiently say, *I'm taking it day by day and doing the best I can every day.*

Patience with your depression-related thoughts and feelings can help you build an internal reservoir of strength and trust in your ability to take care of yourself.

DEFEATING DISTRACTION

Blair is a 36-year-old marketing executive who has a long history of depression. One day, during his weekly therapy session, he wrinkled his face and said in an exasperated tone, "Look, I know you don't give advice and don't have a crystal ball, but when do you think I'll be over being depressed?"

I responded, "You seem frustrated and impatient with yourself about getting better."

Blair reflected that this was the second time he'd distracted himself from his depressive feelings by jumping headfirst into a complicated romantic relationship. He concluded, "Now I'm in over my head, and I guess you're going to tell me that I'm setting myself up for disappointment and depression."

"How does distracting from your depression help you?" I asked.

"I guess it doesn't help me at all. I don't deal with the feelings. I want to feel normal again. Ugh. How do I get myself into this over and over again?"

There's a lot to learn from the discomfort of negative feelings. When you get depressed, the last thing you want to do is set aside time to understand what you may be feeling. It takes support and patience to stay connected with yourself—especially when you're not feeling like your usual self. It wasn't comfortable for Blair to face his depressed feelings. But practicing distress tolerance, reframing his impatient thoughts, and implementing a gratitude practice helped him work through and take charge of a self-defeating pattern that was holding him back. (You'll learn about those techniques in this chapter.) Practicing patience so you can take the time needed to work through your feelings can lead you to independence and agency.

Simple Meditation

Mantra meditations are similar to a seated meditation practice but with the addition of repeating a single word or phrase—a mantra—to quiet down your internal chatter. Repeating a mantra can be helpful because the repetition of a single word helps the mind slow down, stop wandering, and stay in the present. Brain imaging studies have found that the network of brain cells responsible for wondering and worrying about the past and future becomes calm during mantra meditation. This exercise can help you begin your day from a place of tranquility or bring calm when you feel your patience being tested. Spend 3 to 10 minutes on this practice.

1. To perform this exercise, choose a mantra that represents relaxation to you: *peace, calm,* or *completely at ease* are good examples.

2. Sit in a comfortable but alert position, allowing your pelvis to feel firmly planted in your seat with your back upright and head facing forward.

3. Spend the next 30 seconds or so just sitting still, breathing comfortably with your eyes closed (or partially closed).

4. Begin repeating the mantra to yourself, over and over, either aloud or in your head. Thoughts may come into your mind, but just allow the mantra to pull your attention back to the present moment.

Guided Imagery for Developing Patience

Guided visualizations or imagery can be deeply relaxing while also grounding. For people struggling with depression, guided visualizations can help evoke feelings of calm patience. In this exercise, you'll focus your imagination on a location that represents peace to you. It could be somewhere you've been to or an idealized, imaginary location. It might be a natural setting like a beach or forest, a favorite room where you feel safe and relaxed, or a spiritual location like a church, shrine, or temple. Any place that evokes a feeling of calm and tranquility can be your peaceful location.

1. Find a quiet space and get yourself into a position that's comfortable for your body. (This may be sitting up or lying down.)

2. Close (or partially close) your eyes, and breathe deeply into your abdomen, envisioning your peaceful place.

3. Engage all of your senses by imagining how your peaceful place looks, feels, sounds, smells, and even tastes. The more vividly you capture your imagined location, the greater the healing effects of the technique. What colors and shapes do you see? Are there natural sounds, like birds or insects? What kind of surface are you sitting on? Do you smell plants, wood, candles, or incense? Is the air dry or damp? Is there a breeze, or is the air still?

4. Continue breathing from your abdomen. When you notice your mind wandering, patiently bring your attention back to envisioning your peaceful place.

Continue the meditation for as long as you like.

Practice Patience with Distress Tolerance

With this exercise, we'll practice focusing on what gets in our way when we're trying to be patient. Many people with depression find that they have a hard time paying attention; this may feel like impatience, but the root of it can be a difficulty in acknowledging negative feelings, beliefs, or thoughts. This exercise cultivates curiosity and increases your patience and tolerance for uncomfortable feelings.

To begin, you'll need a meaningful or sentimental object, like a picture of a loved one, a favorite work of art, or a memento.

1. Sit comfortably with the object in front of you, and gently focus your gaze on it.

2. Invite and accept whatever feelings or thoughts come up as you gaze at the object.

3. When your mind begins to wander, notice and acknowledge the pull of your thoughts, and ask yourself, *What thoughts and feelings am I avoiding?*

4. After five minutes, list all the thoughts and feelings that were hard to sit with during this exercise.

You may want to try this exercise at the beginning or end of each day. This will help you see patterns more clearly, and you'll begin to develop patience and tolerance for difficult feelings.

Reframing Impatience

In this exercise, you'll give yourself an opportunity to reframe some moments of impatience in your life.

List three recent situations where you found yourself feeling impatient with yourself or with someone else.

Example: *I got frustrated with myself for turning off my alarm and going back to sleep. I am so sick of not being able to get up in the morning.*

In the first column provided, write the impatient thought you had in the moment.

Example: *I'm so lazy. Just get up—it's not that hard!*

In the second column, describe the feeling you had.

Example: *I was sad and feeling frustrated with myself.*

In the third column, reframe the impatient thought into a compassionate, patient thought.

Example: *I'm feeling a lot of anxiety about starting my day. I'll do my best, but I'm going to be gentle with myself and take it slowly in the mornings.*

Impatient Thought	Feeling	Reframed Thought

Take a pause after the exercise to read over your answers and reflect. Which columns were easier to write than others? Which were harder? Which feelings or thoughts were surprising? Which were familiar? What memories or associations came up? What was it like to reframe the "impatient thought"?

ENCOURAGING WORDS

Take a moment to close your eyes and keep your
attention focused just on your breath. Allow your
focus to move your heart as you read the words
on this page. Remember, when things get tough,
you can move forward in small ways, like the way
you are reading one word at a time, right now.
Sometimes you will have good days, sometimes
not-so-good days. The best way to proceed is to
move in small steps, one at a time. Don't worry
about how much you need to do for tomorrow
or what you haven't finished yet. Just read the
words on this page and take it one moment at a
time. Your steps toward recovery, like the words
and pages you read in this book, will add up.
Sometimes you may not even notice just how
far you've come in your growing and learning.
Simply take it one mindful word and one mindful
step at a time.

Relaxation Meditation

When you're depressed, learning to relax and self-soothe is crucial for gaining more emotional balance and patience. The ability to calm down and soothe yourself allows time for important emotional and physical recovery to take place. In this exercise, mindfulness provides a way to relax your mind, whether in the middle of a hectic afternoon or at the end of a long day. If possible, follow up with some self-care to relax your body; take a hot bath or shower, go for a walk, listen to calm music, or do whatever works for you.

Move through the steps of this exercise at whatever pace feels natural and relaxing.

1. Sit comfortably and close (or partially close) your eyes, focusing your attention on your breath.

2. Keep your attention focused on your breath for a few minutes, feeling the sensations of breathing. Allow your breath to come to a natural, comfortable rhythm.

3. Allow the focus of your attention to expand beyond your breathing, noticing your whole body and any sensations that may be arising.

4. Allow your focus to expand further to include anything that makes contact with your skin. Feel the texture of your clothing, the pressure of your body against the chair, and the movement and temperature of air against your skin and hair.

5. Lastly, expand your awareness to include your senses. Pay attention to everything you can hear, smell, and taste.

6. Now reverse this process, bringing your attention inward by focusing only on the inhale and exhale of your breath.

Acknowledgment Practice

Who are your models of being patient? Who's extended the most patience to you in your most difficult moments? Think of someone you respect in your life who you believe exemplifies patience—it could be a relative, a friend, a teacher, a mentor, a colleague, or even a beloved pet. Any living being who's had a significant impact on your life or with whom you've shared an important experience could be a role model to call to mind when it's a challenge to practice patience.

In this exercise, you're going to write an acknowledgment letter (as a practice for you—you won't be sending it). Don't worry about perfect grammar or spelling in your letter, but take your time and be as specific as possible. This exercise is an opportunity to slow down and recognize how patience impacts you and your relationships and explore some qualities of patience you might want to emulate.

Write a letter to your role model of patience in the space provided or on a separate sheet of paper. Follow this template:

→ Address the letter to the person you're thinking of by name.
→ Describe in specific terms how this person exemplifies patience.

    Example: *I'm writing you this letter because you have been so patient with me in the following ways: You gave me advice on dealing with customers at work, you took the time to teach me when I was doing something wrong, and you never got upset even though it took me a long time to be comfortable answering customer questions and taking calls.*

→ State specifically how their ability to be patient has impacted you. Say what you've learned from their example.

Example: *Your patience has made a difference in the following ways: I learned that I could get better at my job if I took my time. I watched how patient you were with customers and other staff and learned ways to handle myself. Your patience made me feel supported and understood as I learned the ropes.*

→ Write three ways you want to work on giving back to yourself and others what this person has given to you.

Example: *My intention is to act with more patience with myself and others by (1) remembering that it's okay to ask questions if I don't understand someone's complaint, (2) not rushing through interactions with customers and staff, and (3) being supportive and patient when training new hires.*

Mindful Moment: Patience

It's important to remember that impatience has a funny way of popping up in discreet ways. It can be difficult to notice when you're being short with yourself because for many of us, it's an automatic way of being. Judgmental thoughts triggered by depressed feelings can lead to impatience and irritation with yourself and others, potentially leading you down a slippery slope of loneliness, isolation, and stagnation. Lack of patience can serve as an avoidance of deeper understanding, keeping others at a distance and keeping us stuck in our depression. Through practicing the mindfulness principle of patience, we can learn to avoid distracting ourselves from our difficult emotions and focus instead on actively engaging with ourselves and others with gentle understanding.

Practicing patience requires a lot of courage and a bit of rebellion. In the modern world we live in, patience can seem downright counterintuitive. We're constantly bombarded with outside stimulation and pressure to do better—and do more—with less and less time available. When you're feeling pressured to feel better quickly, remind yourself that you're allowed to take as much time for your recovery as you need because your mental health is a priority. If the world won't be patient with you, then you don't need the world's approval or permission. At the end of the day, the social media trending topic that you miss or the party you don't get to won't be there to lend you a helping hand when you're down in the trenches of depression. Focusing on all the things you *could* be doing instead of what you're doing right now is a way of distracting yourself *from yourself*. When we practice the mindfulness principle of patience, we spend time with whatever our experience is in the moment. And we make friends with all of our feelings, the good, the bad, and everything in between.

AFFIRMATION

Depression can make it easy to focus on the past and future—who'd want to focus on the here and now when you're feeling terrible? When you're feeling impatient with what's going on in the moment, take a few seconds and place a hand on your heart while repeating the following:

I am doing the best I can.

The best I can do is all I can do.

I accept myself exactly as I am in this moment.

CHAPTER TAKEAWAYS

1. Practicing patience is a way of taking care of ourselves. It allows us to take as much time as we need to accept all of our feelings, both the joyful and the painful.

2. Recovering from depression is a process, and the mindfulness principle of patience allows time for that process to unfold.

3. Focusing on the future is a way of distancing from our present-moment experience.

4. Developing patience with all of our feelings is an act of acceptance and self-compassion.

5. When we practice patience, we're showing our willingness to make friends with our emotions.

CHAPTER SIX

TRUST

The principle of trust in mindfulness involves connecting to an inner confidence and wisdom that comes from paying consistent attention to our thoughts and feelings. Trust doesn't come automatically. It's a quality that's built over time with consistency. Most of us experience trust in the context of relationships with other people: family members, friends, and romantic partners. But trust is also necessary in our relationship with ourselves.

Building self-trust requires paying attention to and caring for yourself in a steady, committed way. By doing this, you develop the confidence that you can be there for yourself no matter what happens. Depression erodes self-trust because it impacts our ability to function normally and makes it hard for us to take care of ourselves. Some people rely on others to make up this gap, but ultimately, we need to learn to trust in ourselves. Cultivating trust requires small, reliable acts of self-care, a practice that over time develops into a deep understanding and trust in our own inner knowing.

The Mindful Way

The mindfulness tenant of trust can help us feel balanced and restore our sense of connection to both ourselves and the world around us. Depression tends to keep us from the things that bring us joy and connection, undermining our confidence to know what our bodies want and need. Without realizing it, we become more and more distant from self-care and other activities that strengthen and nourish us. Mindfulness trains us to take notice of, accept, and meet our wants and needs to rebuild trust in our ability to handle difficult moments.

In his video *The Attitude of Trust*, Jon Kabat-Zinn describes trust this way: . . . *Every time we don't trust ourselves, we can bring awareness to it and remind ourselves that maybe this is a good opportunity to shift from really feeling like we're not able to trust something, to actually trusting it.*

In small, simple ways, we can build confidence and trust in our ability to handle our experiences. Mindfulness brings awareness to the moments when we don't trust ourselves and reminds us to take the opportunity to change our point of view or make a different choice.

Common Mental and Emotional Patterns

Depression can feel like having the rug pulled out from under you. Everything you counted on in life gets turned upside down, and you're left disoriented and questioning what to do. You might think you're doing fine, going to work and getting along with your friends and family. And then one day you can't get out of bed, and you feel incapable of doing the smallest of tasks like take a shower or send an email. The waves of shame and self-judgment that depression activates can take you away from the here and now, leaving you overwhelmed with feelings of dread about the future and self-doubt about past decisions. This cycle can create a sense of uncertainty about whether you're capable of taking care of yourself, expressed in questions like these:

Why should I trust myself to ever do anything to better myself if I'm just going to end up depressed anyway?

Of course I'm depressed again. See, I can't trust myself to be normal like everyone else.

If I think about what I want, I'll just end up getting depressed and messing it up—what's the point?

Thoughts like the ones listed can lead to isolation and despair. The self-judgment, impatience, and self-doubt that depression fuels can get in the way of the very things we need to help us recover and heal.

The mindfulness practice of trust can help you regain your faith in the healthy, capable aspects of yourself. You'll notice when self-doubt and critical thoughts are distracting you from meeting your need for self-care. When you're aware of what you need in the present, you can act accordingly, discerning between options and trusting your decisions. Trusting yourself may look like taking a walk instead of going for a run or eating your favorite take-out for dinner in lieu of cooking. Sometimes the practice of building trust in yourself may be as simple as doing the easier thing when you feel like you "should" do the hard thing. By making these choices you remind yourself that you're still capable of meeting your needs and caring for yourself.

LETTING GOOD THINGS IN

Ava came into my office one rainy Monday, took off her shoes, flopped down on my couch, and said, "Hey, I think I had a revelation!"

I replied, "Really? Tell me more."

Ava went on to describe how her school guidance counselor had told her that with her "okay" grades and SAT scores, she should just apply to the easiest college to get into and hope it would accept her. At first this made Ava feel that she was a nobody, neither smart nor interesting. But she remembered our discussions about using mindfulness to be aware of her emotions, and she stayed with her feelings of anger and being hurt. Then Ava remembered positive and encouraging comments she'd heard from people she trusted and cared about. "I guess trusting is letting good things into your heart again," Ava told me. "It's not easy, but I'm doing it."

Like Ava, you may have parts of yourself that you wish were different. Mindfulness can help you begin the process of building trust in yourself again by accepting yourself no matter what you may be going through. With trust, you can have the courage to claim and own all aspects of yourself. You can even begin to appreciate them and trust that feelings that may be difficult to accept may also provide an opportunity to better understand what you want or need.

Simple Meditation

This exercise can be as brief or intensive as you need it to be (a duration of 2 to 10 minutes is a good starting range). As you practice it, inhale and exhale through your nose to prevent getting light-headed. Contract each muscle group gently, without straining, for 5 to 10 seconds and then release and relax it for 10 to 20 seconds. Follow with a deep breath, allowing your muscles to relax before moving to the next step. If you have an injury or condition that might be problematic for this exercise, check with your doctor before trying it.

Begin by finding a comfortable position, sitting or lying down.

1. Tense the muscles in your face for 5 to 10 seconds. Tighten the muscles in your forehead by furrowing your eyebrows, squeeze your eyelids shut, scrunch your face, and tighten the muscles of your jaw. Then release and relax for 10 to 20 seconds. Take a deep breath before moving to the next step. As you breathe, imagine the air flowing to your face and alleviating any tension.

2. Tense your shoulders, bringing them up toward your ears. Pause for 5 to 10 seconds, and then release and relax for 10 to 20 seconds. Imagine your breath flowing to your shoulder muscles and alleviating any tension.

3. Tense the muscles in both your arms. Pause for 5 to 10 seconds, and then release and relax for 10 to 20 seconds. Take a deep breath, imagining the air flowing to your arms and relieving any tension.

4. Tense your abdomen, squeezing your abs as if you were doing a sit-up. Pause for 5 to 10 seconds, and then release and relax for 10 to 20 seconds. Imagine your breath flowing to your abdomen and alleviating any tension.

5. Tense your hip muscles and buttocks. Pause for 5 to 10 seconds, and then release and relax for 10 to 20 seconds. Imagine your breath flowing to your hips and alleviating any tension.

6. Tense your thighs. Pause for 5 to 10 seconds, and then release and relax for 10 to 20 seconds. Imagine your breath flowing to your thigh muscles and relaxing any tension.

7. Tense your calves. Pause for 5 to 10 seconds, and then release and relax for 10 to 20 seconds. Imagine your breath flowing to your calves and easing any tension.

8. Tense your feet, curling your toes tightly. Pause for 5 to 10 seconds, and then release and relax for 10 to 20 seconds. Imagine your breath flowing to your feet and alleviating any tension.

After you go through the entire set, take a full inhalation, allowing the air to fill your abdomen and then slowly release. Let go of any focus and allow your body and mind to relax. When you're ready, bring your awareness back to your surroundings at your own pace.

Micro-Actions

Small simple actions you can take throughout the day, called micro-actions, can ground you in the present moment as you show yourself some care and compassion. Micro-actions are simple ways to bring you joy and a little bit of ease while also helping you cultivate sustainable habits and build trust in your ability to follow through on your intentions. When you're discouraged by your depression and want to disengage by going on autopilot, micro-actions can help you engage in small acts that shift your perspective and strengthen your trust in your ability to help care for yourself.

For this exercise, integrate some micro-actions into your day, starting with one or two and adding more as your confidence grows. If you like, add your own micro-actions to the list.

Morning

→ Make your bed.
→ Brush your teeth.
→ Take a big stretch.
→ Put away your phone until you've been awake for at least an hour.
→ Other: _____

Afternoon

→ Make a cup of tea or coffee, or treat yourself to your favorite beverage.
→ Eat a healthy snack.
→ Open your blinds or curtains.
→ Take a stretch break.
→ Go for a walk.
→ Other: _____

Evening:

→ Put dirty laundry in the hamper.

→ Take out the trash.

→ Wipe down the kitchen counters.

→ Lay out your clothes for tomorrow.

→ Take a bath or shower.

→ Other: _____

These activities may seem simplistic and minimal, but when you're depressed, the effort it takes to do the little things can feel like a heavy burden.

Micro-Rewards

When you're depressed, you may struggle with finding ways to get or stay motivated. And depression can trigger feelings of low self-esteem, which can lead to low energy levels, leaving you so inactive that you may ask yourself: *Why would I reward myself when I've been doing nothing?* But thought patterns like this are unmotivating and hurtful, leading to a lack of trust in yourself. Rewarding yourself is an act of kindness and compassion: *No matter how bad I'm feeling, I'm going to care for myself in any way I can.* This practice can help build trust and positive self-regard, both of which are important components when healing and recovering from depression.

Start by making a small positive step—the micro-actions from exercise 1 are good examples—and offer yourself a simple and realistic reward afterward, such as the following:

→ Have a dessert of your choice.
→ Do whatever you want for an hour.
→ Plan one night a week where you cook for yourself or take yourself out for a special meal.
→ Take a quiet walk or bath.
→ Choose one day a week to treat yourself to a coffee from your favorite coffee shop.

Micro-Breaks

Often when we're struggling with depression, it can feel as if we're moving through life on autopilot—not really paying attention to how time is passing by. On any given day, the clock can catapult us forward too quickly or make it feel like time is dragging. Planning a micro-break is a way to build trust in yourself by building self-care into your schedule and protecting and exerting control over your time.

Choose one day a week to institute your micro-breaks. On that day, set an alarm to go off once per hour. When the alarm sounds:

→ Take a minute to stretch.
→ Move your body with a short walk.
→ Sit comfortably and notice your breath.
→ Take a sip of water or more if you're thirsty.

Then return to whatever task is at hand.

ENCOURAGING WORDS

Let go of the battle. Breathe quietly and let it be.
Let your body relax and your heart soften. Open to
whatever you experience without fighting.

—JACK KORNFIELD,
*A PATH WITH HEART: A GUIDE THROUGH THE PERILS
AND PROMISES OF SPIRITUAL LIFE*

You are doing great!
When you're depressed, it's easy to get caught up
in all the things you're not doing. That's totally
understandable because depression can lead to low
energy levels and low self-esteem, making it difficult
to stay motivated. The fact that you're reading this
book is a step in the right direction!
Keep going and don't give up!

Micro-Affirmations

Have you ever noticed how the smallest words of encouragement from a friend or loved one can boost your energy and motivation? Well, the good news is that you can actually learn to do this for yourself! Depression can bring up lots of small, negative thoughts; mindfulness helps us notice and recognize them. Micro-affirmations are small declarations that can take the sting out of our negativity, helping you self-soothe, build trust in yourself, and relax. These positive assertions can help heal self-doubt and build trust in your inner strength by reminding you of your value when depression makes it hard to see anything positive about yourself. Add them to your home or work environment, posting affirmations in a visible place so they'll be there when you need them. Start with the following:

→ *Small is better than none.*
→ *Start with what you can do.*
→ *It's okay to take it slowly.*
→ *You're on the right track.*
→ *The hardest thing is doing what feels right for you.*
→ *Mistakes are a part of life; you can always try again.*
→ *I'm here for myself, no matter what.*

Reflection

Throughout this chapter you've had the opportunity to try out many different types of micro-practices. For this exercise, we're going to take some time to reflect on what went well during each practice, what differences you noticed, and what you would like to try differently.

Micro-actions

These actions worked particularly well for me: ....

....

After practicing micro-actions, I noticed that this was different: ....

....

Going forward with micro-actions, I'd like to do this differently: ....

....

Micro-rewards

These rewards worked particularly well for me: ....

....

After practicing micro-rewards, I noticed that this was different: ....

....

Going forward with micro-rewards, I'd like to do this differently: ....

....

Micro-breaks

These breaks worked particularly well for me: ....

....

After practicing micro-breaks, I noticed that this was different: ....

....

Going forward with micro-breaks, I'd like to do this differently: ....

....

Micro-affirmations

These affirmations worked particularly well for me: ....

....

After practicing micro-affirmations, I noticed that this was different:

....

Going forward with micro-affirmations, I'd like to do this differently: ....

....

Mindful Moment: Trust

Depression can make it really hard to trust ourselves because it limits our ability to function in a healthy, positive way. It takes away the ability to pay attention to our needs and engage in the simplest of self-care that we normally do without even a second thought when not depressed. Learning and practicing self-trust form a continual process, one that you've taken the courageous first steps to explore. Remember, with time and consistency, you will find yourself feeling greater clarity about the things you want and need.

Don't forget: Trust isn't automatic; it's something we build up to over time and with consistency. When you're struggling with depression, time can feel like it's dragging. Much like building trust in any other type of relationship, you can begin by doing something small every day, like being present with your feelings or making your bed in the morning.

AFFIRMATION

When you are having a hard time and feeling stuck in self-defeating thoughts, try using this affirmation to remind yourself to trust your inner goodness and wisdom:

My depression is not all of me.

I trust in my unconditional inner goodness and wisdom.

Recovery isn't always easy, and at times it can even feel monotonous. So many people who live with depression feel isolated and alone with their struggle. It's hard to remember that recovering from depression is not a part-time hobby; it's more like a full-time job. Even though you can't see it or feel it, like the sun hidden behind dark stormy clouds, you can trust that your inner goodness and wisdom are shining bright and strong, just waiting to come out to greet you, again and again. By doing the exercises in this chapter, you're building a strong, resilient foundation you can trust. That foundation is you!

CHAPTER TAKEAWAYS

1. Your relationship to yourself is built on consistency, like any other friendship. The more we're able to show up for ourselves, the more likely we are to establish trust.

2. The mindfulness practice of trust can help you notice when your self-doubt and critical thoughts distract you from meeting your need for self-care.

3. Micro-practices are a way to promote self-trust with small acts that demonstrate your ability to follow through on your intentions.

4. Micro-affirmations can be applied to yourself for encouragement, cultivating self-compassion and trust.

5. Focusing on the future and all the things you could be doing is a way of distracting you from yourself.

CHAPTER SEVEN

NON-STRIVING

External goals can keep us motivated and moving forward—but at what cost? If you're always looking ahead, it can be easy to miss what's happening right now. The mindfulness principle of non-striving invites us to connect with the process rather than get attached to the outcome. It's true that striving to reach goals and accomplishments can be rewarding, but at times striving toward an outcome may be a way to escape unwanted feelings. You won't know for sure what's driving all the striving until you slow down to check it out and understand. Striving without mindfulness is like speeding past beautiful scenery to get to the airport . . . so you can move on to what you imagine will be an even more beautiful landscape.

Often, we're sitting with a mixture of pleasant and unpleasant thoughts and feelings, and the unpleasant ones can make us impatient to move on. When you only focus on future goals, though, you're blocking out not only the unpleasant but also the pleasant aspects of the current moment. This can leave you with feelings of emptiness, dissatisfaction, and loneliness. Mindful non-striving can add richness to all aspects of your experience.

The Mindful Way

When you're depressed, working toward external goals can feel like trying to climb a mountain—a never-ending climb that leaves you feeling dissatisfied, empty, and lonely. In our society we're inundated with advertisements and other messages that promise us happiness and success, telling us that the harder we work, the happier we'll be. However, the opposite tends to be true: The harder we push ourselves and the more we put off the present so we can reach some imagined future, the more drained and depressed we feel right now. When we're already struggling with depression, pushing ourselves to meet external goals can exceed our capacities and tap out our resources— keeping us in a seemingly endless uphill battle with our low mood.

But what if reaching the top of that mountain wasn't the most important part? When we practice the mindfulness principle of non-striving, we're focused more on the journey of climbing the hill instead of the goal of reaching the top. Mindfulness itself is a state of being, not a task to check off our to-do list, so practicing it teaches us what non-striving feels like. When we're burdened by depression, non-striving can help us focus on what we're doing without concern about timelines, quotas, or milestones, generating a sense of presence and accomplishment. With non-striving, we fully experience what we're doing instead of focusing on what we "should" get done.

Common Mental and Emotional Patterns

Most of us have been in situations where we've had to complete tasks according to schedules and deadlines. Influenced by our jobs, our family, social media, and society at large, we can easily absorb the language of goal seeking into our internal dialogue. And depression can turn that dialogue into a self-defeating script, berating us with criticisms like:

Why aren't you further along in your career by now?

How come you don't get up at the crack of dawn and work out like everyone else?

You shouldn't be sitting around resting; you should be accomplishing something.

When we're stressed, that script gets even louder, leading us to punish ourselves with harsh criticism or become deflated and weighed down by judgments and hopelessness. Instead of motivating us to get things done, fixating on unachieved goals leaves us feeling unable to accomplish even the simplest of tasks. This internal pressure to strive for more only intensifies the negative feelings brought about by depression.

The most insidious part of all this is that if we constantly strive for "better," we can never feel that we're good enough just as we are. To practice non-striving is to slow down that fast-moving script in order to introduce a more affirming one. You can find pleasure, fulfillment, and joy in what you're doing without the burden of having to be anything other than who you are right now.

Zach works at a successful film production company. He came to me feeling overworked and overwhelmed by unending pressure, both internal and external. "Sometimes I'm moved to tears for no reason at all," he told me. "It's as if all of a sudden, I realize where I am rather than where I was or where I want to be." When encouraged to try out the mindfulness principle of non-striving, Zach was initially reluctant, not wanting to feel the depression and sadness that arise when he steps away from his work.

Zach was eventually willing to try non-striving practices, starting with a simple meditation. After building some tolerance to slowing down and sitting with his thoughts, he moved on to other practices. Zach began to realize that he had been striving at work to run away from feelings of sadness, anger, and failure he's carried since childhood, when he was abused and made to feel unsafe. He reported that the critical thoughts arising during meditation were the ones he heard growing up: *Don't you have anything better to do? Why are you wasting your time doing nothing?* Zach worked on slowing down his thoughts using breathing techniques. He allowed himself to feel the emotions, exploring and resolving his fears with writing exercises like the ones in this chapter. As he grew his awareness of his tendency to run from overwhelming feelings and started facing them instead, he reconnected with the pleasure and joy he felt for his work. He stopped striving endlessly toward a goalpost as a way to escape unwanted feelings.

Simple Meditation

Your mind is kind of like a ship at sea. Your thoughts, when you're over-striving, are like stormy waves that knock your ship off course and make for a turbulent ride. When you practice mindful non-striving, you calm the waves, with your breath as the rudder that keeps you steady. This grounding exercise allows you to stay the course and enjoy the experience of sailing the waves by keeping your mind focused on the rhythmic cycle of your breathing.

1. Set a timer for 5 to 10 minutes. Settle yourself into a position that feels comfortable for your body, either sitting up or lying down. Connect to your breath by noticing the air moving in and out of your nose as you breathe.

2. Count each time you exhale, starting at one.

3. Continue counting on the exhales until you get to 10.

4. When you reach 10, return back to one and begin again.

5. Repeat the cycle of 10 until your timer goes off.

Pay attention to your thoughts when they begin to wander; notice the thought and gently return your attention to your breathing, starting your count from one again.

Four Square Drawing

This drawing exercise is designed to help you get connected with the nonverbal part of your brain, that part of you that processes through imagery and imagination. Creativity can be a wonderful way to better notice, understand, and express our feelings instead of striving for an outcome. And some emotions are easier to navigate when we have paper, canvas, and coloring tools to express them with.

For this exercise, there are four boxes with instructions for what to draw in each. Interpret the instructions however you choose, and create your drawings with whatever materials and in whatever style you like. Your drawings can be simple stick figures or abstract shapes and colors; they can include words or captions or any elements you choose. Don't try to overachieve on this one; your drawing doesn't need look like a van Gogh masterpiece! Practice non-striving by enjoying the act of drawing in the moment without being concerned about meeting some external standard of artistic skill.

In the first box, draw a picture of what happens when you are striving.

In the second box, draw a picture of what it looks like when you're rested and non-striving.

In the third box, draw a picture of what gets in your way or blocks you from non-striving.

In the fourth box, draw what needs to change to actualize what you've drawn in the second box.

1

2

3

4

Loosen the Tension

There are times we can get so focused on achieving that we lose track of the tension that builds up in our bodies. And when our body tenses up, it can be a signal to our mind to ramp up more pressure . . . which leads to more tension in the body and a feedback loop of overdoing it. This exercise is a great way to check in with yourself and disrupt this self-defeating feedback loop!

1. Take some time to get into a comfortable position with your eyes open or closed. Focus your attention on your body, and take note of any feelings of tension or tightness that are present.

2. Mark the figure provided, placing an X on all the areas of your body where you feel discomfort.

3. Choose one spot that you marked on the figure to focus your attention on. How tense or uncomfortable does that area feel, on a scale from 1 (no tension at all) to 10 (maximum tension or pain)? Write the number down on the figure.

4. Focus your attention on that part on your body, closing your eyes if you like. Take a gentle breath in.

5. Exhale slowly through your nose.

6. Bring your awareness back to the body part. On a scale of 1 to 10, how tense does it feel now? Repeat steps 4 and 5 until the tension is reduced to a comfortable level.

7. Repeat steps 3 to 6 until you've cycled through all the tense areas you marked, evaluating the tension until you feel sufficiently relaxed.

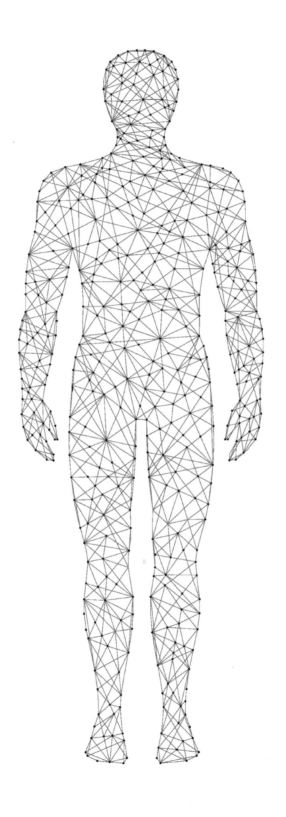

Slow Down Striving Thoughts

Now that you have a sense of how you hold tension in your body, let's practice slowing down your striving thoughts with kind, gentle affirmations. Find a comfortable sitting position, and set a timer for 5 to 10 minutes. You can use this exercise when you are feeling pressured or stressed to reach a goal, or practice it daily as a way to develop a non-striving mindset.

1. For the first minute or so, identify a striving thought that has been building pressure or tension in your body or mind. It may be helpful to think of something you've been needing or feel urgency to do.

2. Observe the thought while noticing any accompanying pressure or tension you feel.

3. In the columns provided, write down some striving thoughts that came to your mind. Then write down a gentle affirmation to replace the striving thought.

Striving Thought	Affirmation
Examples:	Examples:
I have to clean the house before I let anyone come to visit.	*I can clean as best I can and accept my imperfections. My friends won't expect perfection.*
I can't slow down because I have to be prepared for my presentation next week.	*Slowing down will give me a chance to rest, clear my head, and then focus on my preparations.*
If I don't get to the gym today, it will be the third workout in a row that I skipped.	*If I miss another workout, it's okay. I'll take a rest and give myself a break.*

Striving Thought	Affirmation

Striving Thought	Affirmation

ENCOURAGING WORDS

By striving and pushing forward, you can accomplish a few things. But with a non-striving and gentle approach, you can accomplish even more. The strength that develops from mindfully knowing that we have everything we need in the present moment gives us an internal confidence because we are no longer desperate to find validation from the outside. We come to understand that we already have everything we need within, freeing us to engage fully in the present.

Getting to Know Our Fears

Let's explore what may be keeping you from slowing down and feeling fulfilled in the moment instead of relying on external validation in the future. For many of us, the need to be constantly striving is an old protective mechanism or habit from the past. It may be an idea or a belief passed down to you from your parents, teachers, or friends. In this exercise, you'll use the series of reflections to get to know the fears and concerns behind the striving. And maybe you'll even invite some of that stress, anxiety, and fear to come closer so you can give them some notice and care.

1. To start, make a list of things you feel you should do today.

Examples: *respond to work emails, clean the bathroom, schedule a doctor appointment*

_____

_____

2. Pick one task from the list that feels particularly unappealing.

Example: *respond to work emails*

_____

_____

3. What self-defeating thoughts arise when I think about this task?

Example: *If I don't respond to these emails immediately, they'll think I'm a bad employee, and I'll get fired.*

....

....

4. What's the fear behind those thoughts? What are the self-defeating thoughts protecting me from?

Examples: *I have a fear of losing respect and fear of not being liked, which will mean I'm exposed as not good enough.*

....

....

5. Identify healthy non-striving activities that you can do to help ease the stress.

Examples: *commiserate with a friend to talk about how much we both dislike answering work emails after work hours, make a note to respond to the email in the morning and go take a bath, go for a short walk around the neighborhood*

....

....

REFLECTION

Take time after the exercise to reflect about the experience of exploring your fears and concerns.

1. What feelings and thoughts did you have as you were doing this exercise?

....

....

2. What parts of the exercise did you find yourself having difficulty answering? Which questions felt easier?

....

....

3. Did you encounter anything that was different or new?

....

....

Self-Reflective Journaling

Now that you've explored some of your self-defeating thoughts, we're going to try to understand them a little bit better while practicing a self-reflective soothing exercise.

1. Where do you think your striving thoughts come from? Where did you learn to value unhealthy overachievement?

2. What memories do you associate with these thoughts?

3. What insights did you gain about yourself during this exercise?

4. Was there anything that surprised you?

5. What are some new ways you can affirm and comfort yourself when you are feeling pressured and over-striving?

Mindful Moment: Non-Striving

There's a cost to always reaching for never-ending external goals, pressures, and milestones. We do sometimes need external pressures to motivate us. But letting those pressures take over our lives exacts a heavy toll. Looking ahead to where you want to go can help you feel focused and provide purpose. But focusing on nothing else means you're inattentive to a big chunk of experiences that make life meaningful.

Non-striving doesn't mean not trying. When you practice the mindfulness principle of non-striving, you choose to be present in whatever task you're engaged with rather than just crossing it off your to-do list on the way to some far-off objective. When we're struggling with limits imposed on us by depression, non-striving reminds us to appreciate what we're doing instead of focusing on how much we "should" or "need" to get done.

AFFIRMATION

Here's an affirmation that you might want to try repeating to yourself throughout the week as a reminder of mindful non-striving:

It's okay to just be.

CHAPTER TAKEAWAYS

1. Always looking ahead to reach an outcome can mean missing the process it takes to get there.

2. Non-striving can help us focus on what we're doing instead of fixating on what we need to get done.

3. Depression can burden us with self-defeating scripts about unachieved goals.

4. If we're constantly striving for something better, we'll never feel good enough just as we are.

5. When you push and strive, you can get some things done, but non-striving allows you to enjoy the journey and still end up at the intended destination.

CHAPTER EIGHT

LETTING GO

Sometimes we don't even realize how familiar and comfortable we've become with the very things that bring us down. With the principles of mindfulness, we learn to observe and accept the negative thoughts and feelings that we've been avoiding or trying to ignore. In the previous chapter, we discussed non-striving as a way to slow down and take in our experiences, including the negative ones. When you're depressed, especially if you've been struggling with depression for a long while, it may feel impossible to loosen the ties to all the negativity you've been carrying for so long.

Letting it go requires consciously disengaging from the negative thoughts and distortions that you've been clinging to. The mindfulness principle of letting go is also a process of letting in: As you free yourself from habitual negativity, you'll incrementally let in positive feelings and thoughts so you can get used to a different way of being. You don't have to push yourself to be positive; simply allowing yourself to feel grateful for all your hard work can release habitual negative thoughts and make space for appreciation.

The Mindful Way

Letting go of this all-or-nothing thinking is one of the most difficult stages of depression recovery. Most people who are depressed long to feel better. When something helps, even just a little bit, it can be easy to build habitual, negative thinking patterns around that behavior: *If I don't do X every day, I'll become depressed again!* It's understandable that someone struggling with depression wants so badly to feel better that they cling to a particular recovery method or approach as their only hope. But as we saw in the previous chapter, this kind of striving toward an external goal pulls us away from what's happening in the moment. The mindful approach to letting go doesn't mean we resign ourselves to being depressed. Rather, it encourages us to get off the all-or-nothing roller coaster that results when we cling to specific measures of success or methods of managing our depression. When we let go, we open up to other possibilities and more options.

Common Mental and Emotional Patterns

A helpful way to consider the concept of letting go is to think of your mind as a garden. Positive thoughts are like nutritious vegetables and fruits that you're trying to grow. Negative thoughts are like weeds, and as every gardener knows, nothing good grows in a garden overgrown with weeds. So you'll need to weed your garden if you want your nutritious vegetables to grow and thrive. In case you don't know much about gardening, there's a lot of weeding involved! Weeding isn't something you do just once; weeds sprout up all the time, and you have to check in on your garden regularly. If you're too attached to the idea of a perfect garden and approach weeding with all-or-nothing thinking, you'll be overwhelmed and end up exhausted and defeated. Let go of the idea of keeping your garden perfectly weed-free at all times. Just accept that with regular weeding, your vegetables will grow.

Negative thoughts will inevitably pop up:

I'm never going to feel good again. What's the point?

I'm a total failure at life!

I'm so bad at everything I do.

You can't keep them from sprouting. But you don't have to let them take up space and overrun your mind. Notice that they're present, recognize them as weeds, and gently pull them aside. Allow positive thoughts to grow in their place:

I'm feeling bad right now, but feelings don't last forever.

I can do small things to help myself get through this!

I am not my depression, and it doesn't have to define me.

The mindfulness principle of letting go can help you identify unhealthy thought patterns. You can let them go, to make space for more positive, affirming thoughts and feelings that lead to healthy actions. When you practice letting go, you keep negative thoughts and mood-dependent thinking from taking over so you can let in growth and positivity.

Ella came to therapy suffering from bouts of depression, substance dependency, and low self-esteem. She reported feeling sad most of her life and using food and drugs to numb herself. Abandoned at age four and raised by her grandmother, she described how alone she felt growing up, feeling ashamed about not having a family. Ella could never shake the feeling of not being good enough and felt overwhelming shame and inadequacy.

Ella worked hard to implement the mindfulness principle of letting go, which allowed her to get in touch with her loneliness and heal the painful feelings from the past. During a mindfulness exercise she recalled that her critical self-talk sounded very much like the criticisms she heard from her grandmother as a child: "You're not going to amount to anything if you keep being lazy. Why can't you do anything right?" This insight allowed Ella to understand that her negative thoughts were the result of how she'd grown up and were limiting her ability to grow. She practiced mindful letting go exercises and developed supportive thoughts, which allowed for flexibility and self-compassion. Positive affirmations helped counter some of the harsh negative thoughts that contributed to her depression: *It's okay to make mistakes. I can go at my own pace. I am learning and growing every day. I am capable, deserving, and worthy of love.* By spending time mindfully facing the painful feelings of sadness, anger, and shame from her childhood, Ella was able to let go of the past.

Simple Meditation

This unstructured meditation is an opportunity to check in with yourself and reset. First find a spot to sit or lie down comfortably. Set a timer for 5 to 10 minutes. Take a few deep breaths, breathing in and out of your abdomen. Close or partly close your eyes. While taking your deep breaths, do the following:

→ Notice any physical sensations you may be having: tightness or stiffness in your muscles, pressure of your body against your chair or bed, texture of clothing or sensation of air on your skin.

→ Notice the sounds you're hearing.

→ Notice any smells.

→ Notice any sensations of taste.

→ When your mind begins to wander, bring your awareness back to your body and your breathing.

→ Pay attention to any parts of your body that feel tense, numb, or heavy. Note any feelings or thoughts that come up when you pay attention to the tension.

→ Allow yourself to focus back on your breath when your mind begins to wander. Notice the sensation of your breathing and count your breaths, both the inhalations and exhalations.

Continue with the meditation, focusing on your breathing, for long as you want until the timer goes off. Then allow yourself to relax by breathing normally. Stretch and take a moment to reorient to your surroundings.

Wake Up and Refresh Breathing

This next exercise is also called 4-6-8 breathing. It encourages slow breathing that can help calm and bring tranquility to your nervous system. When you're feeling overwhelmed or stressed, this exercise enables you to take a pause so you can come back refreshed and awake with increased energy and more focus. It's also helpful to practice when you're having trouble releasing negative thoughts.

Sit comfortably or stand if you need to. The exercise can be done with your eyes open. Pick a spot in front of you to look at; soften your gaze so that you're not focusing on it intensely.

1. Inhale through your nose and count 4 seconds. As you breathe in, imagine air filling up your lungs and stomach.

2. Hold in your breath for a count of 6 seconds.

3. Slowly breathe out through your nose for a count of 8 seconds.

Repeat three to four times or until you feel more relaxed and at ease.

Clearing Out Internal Clutter

Studies have found that engaging in labeling feelings and writing them out can lower depressive symptoms and increase positivity. Writing about feelings helps you identify what's bothering you and make sense of it. When you understand your difficult feelings, you generate the agency to let go and make space for new experiences. For this next exercise, we'll begin by identifying a painful and unpleasant feeling and the underlying thoughts, beliefs, and memories that reinforce it. Writing your way to deeper understanding can help you let go of the negative clutter that no longer serves you. Fill in the answers in the space provided.

1. The feeling I want to let go of is:

Example: *sadness*

2. The underlying thought I want to let go of is:

Example: *I can't ever do anything right.*

3. The underlying belief about myself I want to let go of is:

Example: *I'm not smart enough.*

4. The underlying memory I want to let go of is:

Example: *I was embarrassed at the last work review when my boss told me all the mistakes I've been making.*

Next, use the space provided to list four experiences that you missed out on because you avoided or distracted yourself from dealing with the issues listed in items 1 through 4.

Now make a list of four replacements for your original list.

I feeling I want is _____.

The thought I want is _____.

The belief about myself I want to have is _____.

The memory I want to have is _____.

Once you've completed the list, answer the following questions:

5. What would I lose by not distracting myself and really letting go of the items in 1 through 4?

6. What does holding on to these beliefs, thoughts, and feelings cost me in my life?

7. What would help me let go of them and have more meaningful and fulfilling experiences?

Letting In the Good

As paradoxical as it may seem, the work of letting go is actually a process of letting in. For this exercise, make yourself a list of qualities, attitudes, beliefs, and feelings you'd like to let into your life. Make as long a list as you can, including everything that's important to you. Examples could include: *love, appreciation, change, growth, care.*

Once you have your list, say each word aloud and then breathe in. As you exhale, notice what thoughts, feelings, and sensations arise. You can try this exercise at the end of each day or at the end of a workweek to practice letting in positive thoughts. Reflect on the following:

1. Which words on the list were easier to let in, and which were more difficult?

2. Did you experience any thoughts or feelings that felt comfortable or uncomfortable?

3. Write down any thoughts or feelings you had during the exercise and reflect on how they may impact your mood and choices you make throughout the rest of your day.

ENCOURAGING WORDS

For many of us struggling with depression, letting in new feelings, experiences, and even joy can be an adjustment. We may be so used to feeling bad that feeling good is a shock to our systems. Just know that over time, with a bit of practice and a touch of patience, accepting our feelings of love, appreciation, hope, and joy can become easier.

Balance Your Thinking

For many people who suffer from depression, the need for comfort and control may lead to *cognitive distortions*. These are patterns of negative thinking that lead us to feel that we have less agency than we do and convince us that we're helpless. The all-or-nothing thinking that we've mentioned earlier in this chapter is one example. Holding on to this type of unbalanced thinking not only creates emotional turmoil and throws us off-center, it causes us to ignore the full range of possibilities that make up the richness of life. We let go of these thinking habits by replacing them with more nuanced, balanced thoughts.

Some examples of unbalanced, all-or-nothing thinking:

I'm not successful, so I'm an utter failure.

I'm a terrible person because I'm not a perfect saint.

I'm not a go-getter, which makes me a passive person.

I'm not strong, so I must be weak.

The balanced version of those thoughts would be:

I can be successful and still have some struggles.

I can feel bad about myself and still be a decent person.

I can be motivated at times; other times, I'm less motivated.

I can feel confident and strong in some situations and need help and support other times.

This exercise is intended to help you identify all-or-nothing thinking and come up with replacement thoughts.

1. Find a comfortable sitting position. You can close your eyes or keep them open, whichever you prefer.

2. Think of an upsetting situation that occurred recently. Take a moment to bring the details to mind.

3. Observe the thoughts that arise. Notice any examples of all-or-nothing thinking and write them down in the space provided.

4. Continue to observe and notice any feelings, thoughts, and sensations that come up.

5. When you're ready to move on, slowly inhale and exhale from your nose. Visualize a favorite safe place, a comforting memory, or a person whom you care about. Notice what feelings, thoughts, and sensations come up.

6. Compose one or more balanced thoughts to replace the all-or-nothing thinking that you documented. Write your balanced thoughts in the space provided.

7. Notice what feelings, thoughts, and sensations come up.

8. Continue to think about the difficult situation that you remembered. Alternate between all-or-nothing thoughts and balanced thoughts about the incident, recording your reflections here or on a separate page if you need more space.

Try to continue step 8 for 10 to 20 minutes, but stop sooner if you need to.

To finish, take a moment to appreciate and thank all your thoughts and feelings, both balanced and unbalanced.

Rainbows after the Catastrophic Storm

When you become more aware of your thoughts and feelings, you may begin to notice patterns in your life that are hard to sit with. Confronted with more negative thinking habits than you realized you had, you may even have the thought, *I guess this means it's hopeless and I've failed at mindfulness.* Catastrophizing is a way to jump to conclusions and assume the worst, and it's a tendency we all have. (Remember the negativity bias we discussed in chapter 3?) When you're depressed, your mind can go into autopilot, leaping to worst-case scenarios that can set you up for disappointment, drive you to try to "fix" the problem in a panic, or just leave you feeling overwhelmed. Depression puts you into a catastrophic storm, raining catastrophic thoughts about everything, convincing you that you'll feel terrible if things don't happen in a certain way. It can even affect the way you think about your mindfulness practice.

Some examples of catastrophic storm thoughts are:

If I can't be happy, I'm going to end up losing my job and be alone for the rest of my life.

I've been doing these exercises for the past six weeks. There must be something severely wrong with me because I'm not 100 percent better.

In this final exercise, we'll tackle catastrophic storm thoughts and find ways to turn them into rainbow thoughts. You can use this process anytime you're feeling negative about your recovery from depression and your practice of mindfulness.

Make your own table using the example on the next page. In the first column, list catastrophic storm thoughts to let go of. Typically these are statements with words like *never, always, awful, ruined, can't,* or *impossible.* In the second column, list an alternative rainbow thought to replace each catastrophic storm thought.

Let Go of Catastrophic Thoughts	Let In Rainbow Thoughts
Examples:	Examples:
I'm always depressed, so I'll never be normal.	*Being depressed doesn't change who I am as a person.*
I can't do math; I am going to fail out of school.	*I have a hard time with math, so I'll work on it, but I'm pretty good at history and English.*

Let Go of Catastrophic Thoughts	Let In Rainbow Thoughts

Let Go of Catastrophic Thoughts	Let In Rainbow Thoughts

When you're finished, consider these reflection questions.

1. What did you notice when you were writing down your catastrophic thoughts?

2. What did you notice when you were coming up with rainbow thoughts?

3. Are there catastrophic storm thoughts that seemed especially hard to let go of? Write them in the space provided.

4. What additional rainbow thoughts can replace those storm thoughts? Write them in the space provided.

Mindful Moment: Letting Go

The mindfulness principle of letting go is a way to release your fixation on the way you think things *should* be and accept them as they *are*. When we're struggling with depression, letting go can be painful because it requires us to face the catastrophizing, all-or-nothing thinking, and other thought patterns we've become accustomed to. Being mindful of our cognitive distortions isn't always pleasant. But when we extend kindness to even our worst thoughts and feelings, we accept and appreciate all aspects of ourselves more fully and deeply. We can give up on punishing ourselves for not being where we would like to be, which is the ultimate act of unconditional love. Letting go can be the most compassionate thing we can do for ourselves.

The mindfulness principle of letting go does more than free you from the cognitive distortions and negative thinking patterns you're used to having. Letting go is a process of *making space* for present-moment experiences. When you let go of the old way of thinking, it can be easier to allow yourself some gratitude and acceptance.

AFFIRMATION

Take a moment to check in with yourself—even if you've started with this chapter, how does it feel to have come this far in your practice of mindfulness? If you're struggling with depression, it can be hard to savor your accomplishments. Give yourself a break, and take a moment to revel in your successes! Allow yourself to let go of any notions about how you "should" be feeling or where you "should" be at, and allow yourself to take a deep breath and be present. Try saying this affirmation, which lets in compassion and support:

Be gentle with yourself; making mistakes is an opportunity to learn and grow.

CHAPTER TAKEAWAYS

1. Letting go is an active process of making space for present-moment experiences. When you let go of the old way of thinking, it can be easier to allow yourself some gratitude and acceptance. Letting go is also a process of letting in.

2. Attachment to the idea that your recovery should happen in a certain way or that it's all wrong is all-or-nothing thinking that sets you up to feel overwhelmed and defeated, like a gardener struggling to eliminate every single weed.

3. Most people who are depressed want to feel better. When they find something that helps, even just a little bit, it can be easy to get sucked into self-defeating thinking patterns in which your recovery hinges on certain practices or methods.

4. Applying compassion to our cognitive distortions, difficult as they may be to acknowledge, can help us let them go and appreciate all aspects of ourselves more fully and deeply.

5. Letting go is a practice to liberate you from depression-related thought patterns.

CHAPTER NINE

ONWARD, UPWARD

Finding What Works for You

At the beginning of this book, you learned that mindfulness is a capacity that everyone has. Now that you've tapped into your superpower of mindfulness, you get to decide the best way to use it.

What I like about mindfulness is that it can be practiced anywhere, anytime, which makes it practical and adaptable . . . not to mention portable! Finding the ways to implement mindfulness that work best for your particular situation may be the most important aspect of an ongoing practice. You can apply mindfulness to your everyday life, but the details are up to you. You've learned to notice your own thoughts and feelings and to trust in your ability to meet your own needs. So you're the expert in what your mindfulness practice can do for you going forward. How would you like to use the skills you've learned in this workbook?

As you develop and personalize your mindfulness practice, here are three important ways to deploy your skills in your depression recovery and beyond.

Situational Coping and Trigger Management

Stressful events will always be part of life, from traumatic losses to life transitions to the demands of work, school, and family. Mindfulness can be used as a way to prepare for difficult times and keep you going through unexpected troubles. As you become familiar with the exercises in this book, take note of which are the most helpful for regulating your mood when you feel stressed. The affirmation and appreciation exercises in chapter 4 can be especially helpful for identifying what situations, people, or events trigger depressive thoughts and feelings so you can manage your moods. When life gets difficult, mindful techniques can help you counter your reactions, preventing and mitigating a potential downward spiral.

Relapse Prevention

Depression can be a slippery slope. Even as we recover, it's like a well-trodden path that we can find ourselves walking without realizing it. For relapse prevention, consider including a small number of mindfulness exercises in your daily routine and making them a habit. Your regular practice might be as simple as applying the mindful eating technique from chapter 2 during one meal every week. Or you might apply the micro-action strategy from chapter 6 by attempting one simple self-care action daily. When you notice a positive habit has fallen out of practice, don't be critical. Take it as a signal that you might be starting to struggle and are in need of more focused mindfulness to maintain your recovery.

Ongoing Self-Care and Self-Actualization

Mindfulness is more than a tool for mitigating depression. As a lifelong practice, it can help you better understand yourself and your relationship with others and develop internal resources to manage stress and stay resilient. As the burden of depression lightens, you may find that you enjoy exploring the possibilities of growth and self-understanding that mindfulness has to offer. Chapters 2 and 8 can help you find meaning and fulfillment as your everyday life becomes open to a new post-depression potential. For example, you might take the same walk every day, but mindfulness shows you that the way the light shines on a flower along the way is different each time. Slowing down to notice what is happening in the moment can allow you to perceive new aspects of yourself, too, including internal resources you didn't know you had. You may think you know yourself because you've spent every day as you are, but by practicing mindfulness you can give yourself the unconditional love and understanding that you may have been missing.

Short-Term Outlook

A key component of an effective ongoing mindfulness practice is trying your best to go easy on yourself. This allows you to be exactly who you are. That may sound simple, but in practice it's not always so straightforward. You may feel pressured to do every exercise in this book or do exercises every day. You may start strong and then fizzle out, with thoughts like *I'm a failure at recovering from depression*. Those self-critical thoughts are a cue to review chapters 5 (patience) and 7 (non-striving). Mindfulness teaches us to do what we can in the moment, not measure how far we've come or how fast we're going. If you feel like you're losing your way, try paring down to one mindfulness exercise and sticking with it until you're more confident.

It takes time to build habits. Notice what works for you, and tailor your mindfulness practice to your particular needs, using the exercises in key moments and tracking the results. For instance, if you know a particular situation—a holiday, a busy time at work, a change in the seasons—tends to activate depressive thinking, try some mindfulness exercises beforehand. Write a journal reflection on the process, including what worked and what didn't. Over time, this ongoing practice will empower you with the best strategies to handle difficult situations. Like studying or practicing a sport, putting in small amounts of work over time will have a significant impact down the road.

Long-Term Outlook

Depression can be cyclical, and relapse is common. It's a condition that needs to be managed in the long term. Mindfulness strategies are effective in addressing the underlying issues but also helping increase awareness of potential pitfalls.

Depression can feel like falling into a deep hole. Initially, your primary focus is just to survive and look for a way out. This is where hope comes in: It's an invaluable tool to help keep us going. Hope can bring great relief, but it's not a strategy for recovery. When you start practicing mindfulness, you begin to notice with more clarity the negative emotional, thought-based, and behavioral patterns that perpetuate and even exacerbate your low mood. Depression coerces us into doing things in a rigid, repetitive way. It's like walking down a familiar street—you may know the route very well but not notice the potholes in your way. With mindfulness, you can learn to slow down and avoid falling into the same old ditch.

Mindfulness allows you to *do* something different, to keep you out of the cyclical behaviors that bring you pain and suffering. With effort and practice, not only can you step around those potholes, you can choose to take another street. Having an understanding of your mental and emotional patterns, the old story lines, and the "shoulds," you can liberate yourself from the chronic feeling of not being good enough. When you choose to be mindful in the moment, you are surrendering your need for the comfort of what's known and familiar. By taking a new, unknown direction, you're demonstrating the ultimate act of self-compassion and self-acceptance.

RESOURCES

The American Foundation for Suicide Prevention offers support and educational material for those who have or are contemplating suicide, or who love someone who has.
1-800-273-TALK (1-800-273-8255)
AFSP.org

The American Psychiatric Association is a medical society whose members work to ensure that persons with mental illness, including substance use disorders, receive humane care and effective treatment. Educational material is available on their website as well as help finding a psychiatrist.
1-703-907-7300
Psychiatry.org

The American Psychological Association is a professional organization of psychologists. Its website explains how psychologists work with you to alleviate symptoms and offers information on how to manage health and well-being while coping with depression and anxiety.
1-800-374-2721
APA.org

The Anxiety and Depression Association of America offers blogs by experts and patients, educational webinars, and help finding support groups as well as information on how to start groups.
1-240-485-1001
ADAA.org/supportgroups

Behavioral Health Treatment Services Locator is a confidential and anonymous source of information for persons seeking treatment facilities in the United States or US territories for substance use/addiction and/or mental health problems.
FindTreatment.samhsa.gov

Care for Your Mind
This site offers advice on what to do if you can't afford therapy along with information on care coordination, access to treatment, veterans, workplace issues, Medicare, and more.
CareForYourMind.org

Depression and Bipolar Support Alliance is a nonprofit organization providing support groups for people who live with depression or bipolar disorder as well as their friends and family.
1-800-826-3632
DBSAlliance.org

Families for Depression Awareness helps families recognize and cope with depression and bipolar disorder to get people well and prevent suicides.
1-781-890-0220
FamilyAware.org

The National Alliance on Mental Illness is the largest grassroots organization devoted to improving the lives of those affected by mental illness.
1-800-950-NAMI (1-800-950-6264)
NAMI.org

The National Institutes of Mental Health is the largest research organization in the world committed to understanding the treatment and prevention of mental disorders.
1-866-615-6464
NIMH.nih.gov

National Sexual Assault Telephone Hotline
1-800-656-HOPE (4673)
RAINN.org/about-national-sexual-assault-telephone-hotline

The National Suicide Prevention Lifeline is a free, 24/7, confidential support for anyone struggling with distress or suicidality.
SuicidePreventionlifeline.org

The Trevor Project

If you are thinking about suicide and in need of immediate support, please call the TrevorLifeline at 1-866-488-7386. Text and chat options available. TheTrevorProject.org/get-help-now

United Way Helpline provides help finding a therapist, health care, or basic necessities.
1-800-543-7709

REFERENCES

American Psychiatric Association. "What Is Depression?" Psychiatry.org. Last modified January 2017. Psychiatry.org/patients-families/depression /what-is-depression.

Frost, Robert. *The Poetry of Robert Frost: The Collected Poems, Complete and Unabridged*. New York: Henry Holt, 1979.

Hanson, Rick. "Take in the Good: Do Positive Experiences 'Stick to Your Ribs'?" Accessed June 30, 2020. RickHanson.net/take-in-the-good.

Jazaieri, Hooria. "Which Mindfulness Skills Can Benefit You?" *Greater Good Magazine*. Published October 16, 2017. GreaterGood.berkeley.edu/article /item/which_mindfulness_skills_can_benefit_you.

Kabat-Zinn, Jon. Published April 23, 2020. "MBSR, the Attitude of Trust by Jon Kabat-Zinn." Mindfulness-Based Stress Reduction. MBSRTraining .com/mindfulness-attitude-trust.

Kornfield, Jack. *A Path with Heart: A Guide through the Perils and Promises of Spiritual Life*. New York: Bantam, 1993.

Koskie, Brandi. "Depression: Facts, Statistics, and You." Healthline. Last modified June 3, 2020. Healthline.com/health/depression/facts -statistics-infographic#1.

Rinpoche, Sogyal. *The Tibetan Book of Living and Dying*. San Francisco: HarperOne, 1992.

Siegel, Daniel J. *Mindsight: The New Science of Transformation*. New York: Random House, 2010.

INDEX

A

Acceptance
  about, 3, 55–56, 70
  affirmation, 70
  and depression, 69
  exercises, 59–63, 66–68
  meditation, 58
  mental and emotional patterns, 56–57
  in practice, 57
Acknowledgement Practice, 84–85
Affirmations
  acceptance, 70
  beginner's mind, 33
  letting go, 147
  Micro-Affirmations, 100
  non-judgment, 52
  non-striving, 126
  patience, 87
  Positive Affirmations, 40
  trust, 105
Appreciation Walk, 63
Attitude of Gratitude, 61–62
Attitude of Trust, The (Kabat-Zinn), 90

B

Balance Your Thinking, 139–141
Beginner's mind
  about, 3, 14, 33
  affirmation, 33
  and depression, 32
  exercises, 19–25, 27–31
  meditation, 17–18
  mental and emotional patterns, 15
  in practice, 16
Belief systems, 8–9
Body Scan, 59–60
Breathing
  Deep Breathing Balloon, 19–20
  Mindful Breathing, 29–31
  Wake Up and Refresh Breathing, 134
Building Emotional
    Understanding, 66–67

C

Catastrophizing, 142–146
Clearing Out Internal Clutter,
    135–136
Cognitive distortions, 139–141
Compassion. See Self-compassion

D

Deep Breathing Balloon, 19–20
Depression
  about, 7–9
  benefits of mindfulness for, 2, 5–6
  management of, 151–154
  professional treatment for, 10
Discernment, 37
Distress tolerance, 78–79
Drawing
  Four Square Drawing, 112–113
  Sharing is Caring, 24–25

E

Eating mindfully, 21–23
Embracing Difficult Feelings, 27–28
Emotional Strength Training, 68
Emotions. *See* Feelings and emotions
Exercise, physical, 63
Exercises, about, 10, 12

F

Fears, 121–123
Feelings and emotions, 9
  Building Emotional
    Understanding, 66–67
  Clearing Out Internal Clutter, 135–136
  Embracing Difficult Feelings, 27–28
  Emotional Strength Training, 68
  5-4-3-2-1 technique, 17–18
  4-6-8 breathing, 134
  Four Square Drawing, 112–113
Frost, Robert, 64–65

G

Getting to Know Our Fears, 121–123
Goals. *See* Non-striving
Gratitude
  Attitude of Gratitude, 61–62
  Thank-You Note to Yourself, 50
Grounding exercises,
    17–18, 39, 58, 111
Guided Imagery for Developing
    Patience, 77

H

Habit-building, 153
Hanson, Rick, 36
Hungry Monk, 21–23

J

Judgment. *See* Non-judgment

K

Kabat-Zinn, Jon, 3, 90
Kornfield, Jack, 99

L

Letting go
  about, 4, 129–130, 148
  affirmation, 147
  and depression, 147
  exercises, 134–137, 139–146
  meditation, 133
  mental and emotional patterns, 131
  in practice, 132
Letting In the Good, 137
Loosen the Tension, 114–115

M

Making space. *See* Letting go
Mantras, 76. *See also* Affirmations
Meditations
  acceptance, 58
  beginner's mind, 17–18
  letting go, 133
  non-judgment, 39
  non-striving, 111
  patience, 76
  Relaxing Meditation, 83
  trust, 93–94
Micro-Actions, 95–96
Micro-Affirmations, 100
Micro-Breaks, 98
Micro-Rewards, 97
Mind-body connection, 2, 8

Mindful Breathing, 29–31
Mindfulness
    applying, 151–154
    benefits of for depression, 2, 5–6
    defined, 1
    principles of, 3–4
    as a process, 11
Mindfulness-based stress
    reduction (MBSR), 3

N

Negativity bias, 36–37. *See also*
    Positivity Bias
Non-judgment
    about, 3, 35–37, 52
    affirmation, 52
    and depression, 51
    exercises, 40–45, 47–50
    meditation, 39
    mental and emotional patterns, 37
    in practice, 38
Non-striving
    about, 4, 107–108, 125–126
    affirmation, 126
    exercises, 112–119, 121–124
    meditation, 111
    mental and emotional patterns, 109
    in practice, 110

P

Patience
    about, 4, 73–74, 87
    affirmation, 87
    and depression, 86
    exercises, 77–81, 83–85
    meditation, 76

mental and emotional patterns, 74–75
    in practice, 75
Positive Affirmations, 40
Positivity Bias, 42–45
Practice Patience with Distress Tol-
    erance, 78–79
Professional treatment, 10

R

Rainbows after the Catastrophic
    Storm, 142–146
Reflection, 101–102
    Self-Reflective Journaling, 124
Reframing Impatience, 80–81
Relapse prevention, 152
Relaxing Meditation, 83
Rinpoche, Dilgo Khyenste, 72
Rituals, 47–49
"Road Not Taken, The" (Frost), 65

S

Self-compassion, 11
    Self-Compassion Reset, 41
    Self-Compassion Ritual, 47–49
Self-Reflective Journaling, 124
Sensory grounding, 17–18
Sharing is Caring, 24–25
Slow Down Striving Thoughts, 116–119
Stress, 9, 56, 109, 152

T

Thank-You Note to Yourself, 50
Thoughts. *See also* Letting go
    Balance Your Thinking, 139–141
    cognitive distortions, 139–141
    negative, 8–9, 129–131

Thoughts *(continued)*
   negativity bias, 36–37
   Rainbows after the Catastrophic
      Storm, 142–146
   Slow Down Striving
      Thoughts, 116–119
Trauma, 9, 12
Trigger management, 152
Trust
   about, 4, 89–90, 105
   affirmation, 104

   and depression, 103
   exercises, 95–98, 100–102
   meditation, 93–94
   mental and emotional patterns, 91
   in practice, 92

V

Visualization, 77

W

Wake Up and Refresh Breathing, 134

ACKNOWLEDGMENTS

There are so many people who helped me bring this workbook to fruition. First and foremost are my mentors and teachers Dr. Michi Rose, Dr. Phyllis Rauch, Dr. Elliot Zeisel, and Dr. Michael Brook. Thank you for giving me the courage and the push to take my first writing steps.

I'd also like to thank everyone at Callisto Media. It is a pleasure to work with such a professional and efficient team. I am so grateful to my colleagues Madeline Stein and Zoe Roben for their thoughtful insights that helped ground me to write during an unprecedented pandemic. I couldn't have done it without you.

I'd like to add a special note of appreciation for my Monday and Thursday training group. Thanks to all my patients who provided the impetus to translate my clinical understanding into a workbook. And a special thanks goes to my hardworking clinical associates at Mindful NYC in helping me become a more mindful leader by holding me accountable to practice what I preach.

And last but not least, I'd like to thank my family and friends for their support of this project. To Myla, Nietzsche, and Plato, thanks for giving me the much-needed break for play and sunshine. To my friends Barbara Mitchell, Jacqueline Ambrosini, Cassie Chow, and Jenn Hill, thanks for your supportive friendship and listening ear. To my Maui Ohana: Mom and Dad, Marla and John, Greg and Heidi, thank you for keeping me grounded and well-fed. In particular, I'd like to thank my husband, Arben Kane, for being my most dedicated, loving, and enthusiastic fan. Your unwavering faith and belief in me give me the courage to pursue new and exciting endeavors.

ABOUT THE AUTHOR

Yoon Im Kane, LCSW, CGP, is the founder and CEO of Mindful Psychotherapy Services, an outpatient therapy center with offices in Brooklyn and Manhattan. Trained at Yale University, Yoon has been providing treatment as a psychotherapist for more than two decades. She is also the founder of Mndlink, Inc., a remote therapy platform that securely connects therapists with patients. Yoon is a frequent keynote speaker and national presenter on the topics of mindfulness, group psychotherapy, and women's leadership. Currently, Yoon divides her time between Manhattan and Maui. She enjoys spending time with family, trail running, oil painting, and meditating with her two Nigerian dwarf goats, Nietzsche and Plato. You can follow Yoon on all social media platforms at @mindful_nyc.

CPSIA information can be obtained
at www.ICGtesting.com
Printed in the USA
JSHW050345081220
10105JS00003B/13